I0048532

CLIMB

the risks and rewards of elevating your brand

A marketing trail guide for local businesses

JEREMY LADUKE

Climb: The Risks and Rewards of Elevating Your Brand. A Marketing Trail
Guide for Local Businesses
First edition
© 2023 by Jeremy LaDuke

All rights reserved. No part of this publication may be reproduced, distributed, or transmitted in any form or by any means, including photocopying, recording, or other electronic or mechanical methods, without the prior written permission of the publisher, except in the case of brief quotations embodied in critical reviews and certain other noncommercial uses permitted by copyright law. For permission requests, write to the publisher at the address below.

Published by Epic Nine Marketing
556 East Broadway Ave
Maryville, TN 37804
info@epicnine.com
epicnine.com

ISBN: 979-8-9904187-0-7

Printed in United States of America

Contents:

Acknowledgements:

This book could never have happened without my community. These lessons and the inspiration for the story of Marley's are the product of over 20 nearly of working with local businesses and nonprofits, hearing their struggles, and being granted the privilege to help them in various capacities (as a marketer and as a community member) to grow and thrive. To our clients: I hope you see a little of our journey together in the story of Marley's and I hope it inspires you to set your goals even higher for your next mountain.

I would never have had the opportunity to work with the organizations I have or learn those lessons if were not for the incredibly talented group of scrappy marketers at Epic Nine: Marketing Outfitters. I truly believe we have one of the most dynamic and creative agency teams in our region and I am incredibly grateful that I get to work with them. To Derek, Jess, Kaeli, Kayle, Laura, Levi, Linna, Nadiia, Nic, Nicole, Rebecca, Shirl, and Tony - here's to all the mountains we've conquered together and the bigger ones yet to come! A special thanks to Will for designing the cover art for the book and Tonia for pushing me to write this and graciously entertaining the craziest of ideas on a regular basis.

Thank you to those who gave of their time to read the rough draft and tell me how to make it better.

To Pinkie, Morgan, Nathan, and Pax,

Your support and encouragement keep me going, day in and day out. Through every challenge and every celebration, knowing I have you makes all the difference. This one's for you – thanks for being my biggest fans and my favorite people.

INTRODUCTION

If you are reading this, then there is a good chance that you either operate a local business in your community or you are thinking about starting out on that entrepreneurial journey. If so, thank you. I believe that local businesses are the lifeblood of our communities across the country, providing gainful employment to millions of Americans and giving our towns and cities a unique identity that resists the pull to become a monotonous pattern from sea to sea of big box stores and chain restaurants.

The reality is, running a local business is hard work. I know because I started one in 2013. Epic Nine Marketing Outfitters was born out of a passion for great marketing and a desire to see great business thrive. However, passion and will power alone didn't guarantee an easy climb to the top of our mountains. At times, it felt like we were scratching and clawing our way through bills, taxes, HR issues, and more to survive. And after more than a decade of climbing alongside our clients, I learned that we were far from the only ones that have, at one point or another, struggled for survival.

According to the Bureau of Labor, only 50% of new businesses survive past their 5th year. It's my hope that this book can help you survive the small business death count and thrive.

Your marketing is the engine for your business. If you don't understand engines or know how they work, then attempting to fix a broken one is a daunting task. I tried to restore a '64 Super Beetle once. It caught fire. If I had more time, better instructions, and possibly better tools, then the outcome might have been different. If I had known the pitfalls to watch out for (like spilling gasoline near the spark plugs when replacing the fuel filter), then I might still be squeezing myself into a tiny classic car with pride. I want to help you avoid the pitfalls and maximize the profits of your marketing efforts and avoid burning down your business with marketing mistakes.

You might have noticed that I used the term 'local business' earlier. I use the term 'local business' instead of 'small business', because I believe it better describes our situations. There are small businesses that are national brands. There are small businesses that are in your community that you might never know about. A local business however, has roots in the local community and is invested in the people, organizations, and future of that community. Furthermore, local businesses face challenges that national brands do not. Marketing is one of the biggest of these challenges. We've all seen great local businesses that have failed. They had an amazing product or service, but they didn't know how to market it. And it's hard to blame them. Marketing is risky business. Literally. Nothing is guaranteed with your marketing. Adobe, the creators of Photoshop, once had a creative ad campaign that depicted a business person going to see a psychic. The marketing executive sits down at a table. The psychic begins to lay out Tarot cards in front of him and asks, "what are the answers that you seek?" To which he nervously responds, "I want to know if my marketing plan is working." The psychic lays down a few more Tarot cards and responds with a smile on her face, "Yes, yes. It's working!" The man looks slightly relieved, but then concern shadows his face again. "Can you be more specific?" The psychic, slightly annoyed, points to two separate cards and says, "Some parts are working. Some parts are not working... That will be $85. Cash only."

This ad comically captures the anxiety many local business owners have about their own marketing. They will invest hard earned money into newspaper, radio, and sometimes TV ads. They'll pay a local freelancer to 'get them to the top of Google'. They might even buy a billboard. But at the end of the day it's hard to say which, if any, of that is working. And it's a wild west type of world out there. There are no government agencies that issue marketing, web design, or branding licenses to make sure they know what they are doing and doing according to established standards. At Epic Nine we've heard versions of the following story hundreds of times. You might even have your own!

"I paid (insert local or national marketing company) thousands of dollars and I didn't see anything from it."

I get it. Even we get the annoying robocalls saying that we 'need to update our free Google listing'. Scammers are everywhere. (For more on the risk of outsourcing your marketing see chapter 3, The Risk of Outsourcing) Sometimes they are easy to spot. Sometimes they come disguised as a reputable national brand. Sometimes, it might even be a friend. They may not realize that they are taking advantage of you. They might be a good person who is just bad at marketing.

This book is intended to be a field guide for you to reference often as you make your way through the marketing wilderness that all local business owners face when trying to grow their brand. It will help you assess the riskiness of a marketing tactic, recognize how to avoid the pitfalls that many businesses get caught in, and understand how to maximize the profits from utilizing it in the right way. The knowledge in this book is hard won from over a decade of helping our clients conquer their marketing mountains. Chapter 1 covers marketing fundamentals and guides you through a Base Camp assessment. The following chapters will each address a particular marketing risk or a marketing mountain. Each chapter will give you a map to help you determine if a particular risk is worth taking, or tools to conquer a marketing mountain. This guide is written so that you can read them in order, hop around, or simply read the one that is the most important to you now. However, I believe you will find a lot of value in the collective wisdom of the whole book.

From chapter to chapter, we will also follow a fictional local business owner as she navigates the path through a business and career transition. Her exact situation may not apply to you, but with a little imagination you will be able to visualize how these principles can apply to your business.

A final of word of encouragement before we begin our journey:

As a local business owner, it's essential to shift your perspective from seeing your enterprise merely as a small business to recognizing it as a **brand**. This change in mindset is not just a semantic play but a powerful strategy for growth and success. Your business, no matter its size, embodies a unique story, a distinct set of values, and a specific promise to your customers. By thinking of your business as a brand, you elevate it from being just another local player to becoming a potential market leader.

Embracing the identity of a brand empowers you to meticulously craft every interaction with your customers, ensuring that each touch point reflects the quality and character of your business. This brand-centric approach fosters loyalty, sets you apart from competitors, and paves the way for scalable growth. Remember, every major brand today once started as a small business. Your journey towards becoming a recognized brand begins with this pivotal change in mindset, where you see your business not as a small entity confined by its current size but as a burgeoning brand with limitless potential.

Day after day, local brands face the immense challenge of competing against the vast budgets and resources of national and international giants. Through this book, my hope is to unlock the strategies and principles employed by these large, successful brands and make them accessible for you so that you may conquer your mountains and elevate your brand.

CHAPTER 1: BASE CAMP

E va paced the waiting room floor outside of the surgical unit. She knew her dad was under a lot of stress with his business, but she never imagined it would cause his heart to fail him. After what felt like an eternity, his physician came into the waiting room and found her. Seeing the concern on her face he reassured her saying, "Your dad is going to be OK." Eva could breathe again. He continued, "But I am surprised he wasn't in here sooner! He had a lot of blockage. We were able to get an emergency stent put in, but he is going to have to have some major lifestyle changes. Food, workload, exercise, the whole gamut." She nodded, her head still swirling with thoughts of what could have happened. He let her know that her dad was in recovery and one of the nurses would come and get her when she could see him.

She sat down, relieved that he was OK, but heavy with the changes she knew were going to have to happen. She and her brother had been pushing for their dad to retire from his business. It wasn't making as much money as it used to and he just wasn't able to keep up with the changing times. But he was too stubborn to just cash it in. He had put his life into that store. In fact, just that year, it was named Burlington's Favorite Downtown Shop. Burlington, Georgia was your typical southeastern small town with a mix of boutiques, antique shops, and offices, along with several vacant buildings that long for someone with some courage and dreams to breath life back into them. But it wasn't a surprise to anyone that lived there that Marley's won. It is a unique store with rare used books and thoughtful toys that, among other things, didn't have screens. It was the type of store you feel accomplished for discovering on a weekend trip to a new town.

When Eva and her brother were kids, they would spend hours with their dad at the shop, playing with the demo toys. In high school they both served their obligatory sentence as shop keeper's child and worked the register in the evenings and during the summer. After high school, Eva went to the University of Georgia and studied business and marketing, mainly because she didn't know what else to do. For one of her classes the final project was to build a website. She chose her dad's business. He didn't have one, so he let her and her group put together a website that looked like what most design-by-committee projects looked like. A few years later, a national marketing company, known for its phone book ads, convinced her dad to invest in a new website. Since then, not much had changed on it other than the store hours.

While she wasn't great with the design side of marketing, she loved the strategy of business and marketing and she was good at it. She landed an internship that turned into a job with a regional hospital in the neighboring city as the PR and marketing director. She had come a long way from bagging puzzles and collector's edition books.

But life has a way of shaking you up, just when you get comfortable.

UNDERSTANDING THE RISKS

"Everyone knows what climbing Mount Everest costs; but only a few know what it is worth." - Reinhold Messner

If getting to the top of Mount Everest was a certain outcome for every climber, then it wouldn't be such a rare thing to do it. However, there have been over 300 deaths from climbers attempting to conquer the summit. Currently there are roughly 200 corpses still frozen to the side of the mountain that have not been removed due to the difficulty of retrieving and removing them, an ominous warning to would be summiters.

As drastic as that is, it only accounts for less than 1% of the number of people who have attempted to climb Everest throughout the years. In comparison, more than 20% of new businesses fail during their first 2 years. Creating a successful business is a treacherous journey. That's why understanding the risks as early as possible is vital to surviving its merciless slopes. You can't get up this mountain with zero risks. There will be points along the way where you will have to spend money, try something new, or trust someone in order to move closer to the summit. And just like mountain climbing, you can't stand still. You can't hunker down and refuse to risk. If you refuse to risk, you will soon run out of resources and options. In business, as in mountain climbing, you have to continue moving forward or you will be falling behind. It's the purpose of this book to help you plan your route to the summit, avoid the pitfalls of sloppy marketing, and realize the profits of exceptional creative and strategic efforts.

No matter how good a potential marketing tactic looks, there will always be risks. Even if it's a marketing tactic that similar businesses in similar markets are using, there is still a risk that it won't work in your business's scenario, because as similar as your situations may be, you are in a unique place, with a unique audience. That 'best practice' might get you some new business, but you are risking just being average, when you could be truly great.

"Unless your advertising is built on a BIG IDEA it will pass like a ship in the night." - David Ogilvy, How to Create Advertising that Sells

That being said, you don't have to bet the farm on your marketing tactics. Very rarely, if ever, will you need to make a marketing decision that could risk you losing your business. Hopefully, by the end of this book you will be able to put the risks in perspective and make smart and bold decisions that help you conquer your marketing mountains.

Marketing Fundamentals

Before a climber makes an ascent of Mt. Everest, she will spend time at the Everest base camp to prepare. In fact, the trek to the base camp is itself a bucket list item for many people with its own challenges. While the summit of Everest is a staggering 29,031 feet, base camp is over halfway there at 17,598. If you've made it a few years in your business, you might look back on that journey as your own Base Camp Trek, and today you find yourself preparing to scale your business up a mountain larger than you've ever faced before.

For Everest climbers, Base Camp is a place for not only acclimatization to high altitude but intense planning and information gathering about local weather and terrain conditions. Weeks can be spent at Base Camp waiting for the right conditions to make an attempt of climbing Everest.

At Epic Nine we have developed a Base Camp Consultation process to assess what the best next steps are for our clients, rather than throwing a bunch of options at them and letting them figure out what they need on their own. Before they can conquer Everest, some businesses need to conquer smaller mountains. Sometimes when they come to us, they aren't sure what their goals should be and so it's hard to determine what mountain needs to be climbed first. You might be in that position, where business has just worked for you for the most part; things have grown at a steady pace and you either got lucky with the marketing you've used, or you've had great word of mouth referrals that have kept you busy. But now, the things that used to work just aren't working as well as they used to. You know you have a top notch service, but the new competition in town is marketing better. You feel the pressure to try something new, but it's hard to know what to try, how much to spend, or who to trust with it. Or perhaps you just need to grow beyond what your current marketing is doing for you. All of these things are valid reasons for a little bit of entrepreneurial anxiety, and it is my hope that by the end of this book you have clearly defined goals and know what your next steps should be.

Before you begin to explore which marketing risks you need to take, it's good to assess your current terrain, look at the weather patterns of the market, and plan your route to the summit. For any map to work for a mountain climber, you first have to orient yourself to your location on it. A good way to start doing that is by completing a SWOT analysis.

SWOT Analysis

A SWOT analysis examines your business's strengths, weaknesses, opportunities, and threats. To complete a SWOT analysis thoroughly requires some honesty and vulnerability. You don't want to gloss over weaknesses or threats. If you build the rest of your marketing on a shaky foundation, then it is very likely that you could compromise your business. Ask your staff and customers that you trust will give you honest feedback.

Your strengths are:

- Things your company does well. In what areas does your company excel? Do you have great customer support? Are you very present in your community? Is there a particular product or service that customers tend to rave about more than others? Make a list of these things.

- Qualities that separate you from the competitors. This is where honesty and vulnerability are important. We all would like to think we are doing everything better than our competitors, but more often than not there may only be 1 or 2 significant areas where we outshine our competition in a meaningful way.

- Internal resources such as skilled, knowledgeable staff. Have you carefully curated the team around you? Are they amazing? Then they would definitely be listed as a strength. I tell people all the time that our team is our company's greatest asset. One of our clients intentionally recruited some of the best product development engineers and spent over a decade perfecting the processes that allow them to turn prototype projects around with lightning fast speed without sacrificing quality. It's a huge strength for them.

- Other strengths might include intangible assets such as intellectual property, proprietary technologies, or your brand's reputation.

Your weaknesses are:

- Things your company lacks. For the first 6 years of Epic Nine our team was stretched thin and all the support requests for websites flowed through me. It was a bottleneck that made my life stressful and our customer support less than desirable. Our lack of staff to efficiently handle the full scope of what we were doing was a big weakness.

- Things your competitors do better than you. Again, honesty and vulnerability are your best friends here. As much as it might hurt to admit it, your competition does at least one thing better than you. If not, then you are in a very very lucky position. However, when you can admit this type of weakness it can lead to opportunities for improvement or perhaps an opportunity to cut out dead weight. They may be beating your product quality, or a particular service that isn't your forte. Cutting it out of your business might free up valuable resources for the things that make you money.

- Resource limitations. All of us have finite resources of money and time. If these are stretched too thin, then they can be a liability.

- Unclear unique selling proposition. If you don't have something that makes you stand apart from the competition, then it is difficult to convince people to choose you.

- Under utilized marketing channels. This is probably one of the most common weaknesses. Are your social media profiles in desperate need of attention? Is your website dated? If you have viable marketing options available, but you aren't using them, then it's a weakness. The good news is that many weaknesses, especially this one, can easily be turned into opportunities.

Your opportunities might be things like:

- Under-served markets for specific products. Drive around the communities you serve, put yourself into the shoes of your target audience and search for vacuums. Is there a particular part of town that doesn't have a go-to service provider for what you offer? Look for niche situations where the demand is higher than the supply.

- Few competitors in your area. If you are the de facto top of mind business in your industry because of a lack of competition then get it while the getting's good! It won't always be like this. Competition will come, but right now there is an opportunity for you to solidify your dominance and deter would be competitors from entering your market.

- Emerging need for your products or services. Is there a need for a new product or service that no one is offering, or perhaps even invented yet? Offering new products not only lets you differentiate yourself from your competition, but it also helps secure your spot as a thought leader in your industry. If creating a new product isn't an option, then you may want to look to industry trade shows. They can be a great resource for finding new products and building relationships with innovative vendors.

- Press/media of your company. Have you done something noteworthy lately (like that new product you invented)? Then get some good press for it. You don't want to bug reporters and media contacts with boring 'news', so reserve your use of this opportunity for justified situations. Some things that might garner you some 'free' press are sponsorships, new community initiatives your business is involved in, new significant hires, or events that your business is hosting. Getting mentioned in the local paper, the evening news, or an industry publication is a great way to build your business's credibility.

And your threats can be:

- Emerging competitors. There will always be new competitors. Keep an eye on them. It's the ones that you think will never make it that can become the most challenging.

- Changing regulatory environment. Is your industry regulated by the government? Then changes in policies can threaten your bottom line at worst, or at best, suck away time to learn the new system and implement changes within your business to accommodate it.

- Negative press/media coverage. The press giveth and the press taketh away.

- Changing customer attitudes toward your company. Is there a service or product that you provide that is harmful to the environment or have any of your employees hurt the company's reputation? If you are on the wrong side of a situation in your community or in the larger culture, then it can threaten your company's reputation.

This is by no means an exhaustive list of SWOT variables, but hopefully it's enough to get your wheels turning. As you conduct your own SWOT analysis be sure to do it in pencil, because as you get through the elements you might be reminded of things that apply and inform the sections that came earlier. Once you've identified these things, you are in a good position to set some goals.

Scan this QR code (theclimb.guide/swot) to find resources that will help you map out your SWOT Analysis.

SMART Goals

If you haven't identified your marketing goals for this year, don't worry, you're not alone. Many of the businesses that come to see us don't have measurable marketing goals either. Some are lucky and business has just worked for them without having to really identify goals. Some aren't so lucky. And when I say 'lucky' I mean it in a literal sense. If you don't have goals and you aren't actively pursuing them and measuring your progress, then you have no real way of knowing if you're heading in the right direction with your marketing. Setting goals is imperative for the success of your marketing. Please do not read any chapters beyond this one before identifying your goals. Once you know your goals, they act as a filter to view all of your marketing options through. Those options either help you reach that goal or they don't. Some help you reach it faster, cheaper, and more efficiently than others. We've seen business owners with no marketing goals other than 'to make more money'. They tend to chase after the shiny new thing, thinking it will answer all their marketing woes. It won't.

In contrast to a goal like 'make more money', your goals need to be specific, measurable, achievable, relevant and time-bound or SMART.

Specific:

By specific I mean something that is as clear and detailed as you can reasonably get it in this setting. It's the difference between "make more money" and "we want to increase our revenue by 20%" or "we want to increase the number of repeat customers by 50%". Being specific forces you to determine things like, which products or services make you the most money with the least amount of effort and what sort of growth opportunities are available to you. Being specific with your goals is the foundation of thinking strategically about the future of your business. When you are determining a specific goal, also determine a specific person that will bear the responsibility for making this happen. Without a leader to accomplish the goal it will just be a great idea that dies in the conference room. That leader might be you. It might be one of your team members. Either way, without some measure of accountability, you shouldn't expect to reach your goal.

Measurable:

SMART goals are also measurable. This means that there are numbers you can put on paper detailing what your current situation is and what you want your future situation to be. "This quarter we had 50 repeat customers, next quarter we want to have 75". One way to easily track your online marketing is through Google analytics and possibly call tracking. If your website, social media, and any paid advertising are set up correctly, then you can track the effectiveness of some campaigns down to the dollar. I should note that tracking your marketing isn't quite the same as having a measurable goal, however there may be elements of your marketing that you want to track and measure throughout the year to ensure you are on track to reach your goals. But while performance marketers and 'growth consultants' tend to laud tracking as the end all and be all of marketing, brand building is less trackable but equally important (more on this in Risk #9).

Achievable:

Being achievable means that this is not some sort of bet the farm, shoot for the moon, marketing gimmick to save your business from bankruptcy. To determine achievability for your business, look at your current situation, your business's past experience and successes, and then make a reasonable estimate of what your growth might look like. Obviously this is something that has a lot of factors involved so it's not an exact science. The goals you set for later in the year may need to be adjusted based on the performance of your marketing in the first part of the year.

Relevant:

Relevancy means that it feeds into the overall goals of the organization which on some level or another is probably to make money. So, while having a social media video 'go viral' would be really cool, it might not actually be a goal that leads to more sales and is probably a bad idea to pursue it as a marketing objective.

Time-bound:

And lastly, SMART goals are time-bound. You are giving these goals a deadline. We all love deadlines, don't we? No, most of us, the sane ones of us, hate deadlines. However, their efficacy is undeniable. And if we were to name them accurately, they would really be life lines for our business because the better and more effectively we can meet them the more likely our businesses are to live.

Examples of some SMART goals are:

- Increase the number of monthly recurring customers by 10% within the next 6 months.

- Generate 10 new leads per month from the website within the next 3 months.

In order for you to reach those goals you will need to take a deep look into who you are trying to reach. So, before we jump into all the marketing tactics ahead of you we need to determine who your target audience is, what is their lifetime value to your business, and what the customer journey looks like for them.

Target Audience:

You might have one target audience or you might have a few for the different products or services you offer. The purpose of defining your target audience is to help you not waste your marketing dollars on people who won't be great customers for you. If you don't aim at anything, you will hit it every time. Defining who you are trying to reach helps you win the best customers for your business. In order to determine who your target audience is, imagine the one customer that, if you could, you'd clone and make all your customers just like him or her. That's the customer that's easy to work with, doesn't flinch at your pricing, and keeps coming back for more. Maybe you have a few of those. What type of person is that?

To help visualize your target audience, you can build out a persona of what a typical in that target audience looks like. The persona might include age, gender, interests, hobbies, pet preferences, lifestyle preferences, income, and more.

Figuring out the persona of your target audience is a way of ignoring the forest and looking at what a single tree might look like. It means cataloging as many details about that tree as you can with the awareness that this tree is not going to look exactly like any other tree in that forest, but understanding that most of the trees share a lot of these same characteristics with the tree you are cataloging.

Target marketing allows you to focus your marketing dollars and brand message on a specific market that is more likely to buy from you than other markets. This is a much more affordable, efficient, and effective way to reach potential clients and generate business. Developing an understanding of who your target audience is will help you answer questions that will inform how you implement your marketing. Consider the implications of how the following information might influence how you conduct your marketing:

- Your target audience is 16-25. What social media platforms will be most beneficial for you?

- You can pinpoint your best clients to a few areas of town. Will this make billboards or direct mail a better option?

- Perhaps you know certain events where you would find your target audience. Would sponsorship or possibly geo-fenced digital ads at the event make more sense?

The calls to action (CTAs) and information about your business can be crafted to address the things your target audience cares about. The CTAs below lean into particular mindsets of target audiences and speaks their language in a captivating way:

- Local Bakery:

  - "Indulge Your Sweet Tooth! Order a custom cake just for you, today!"

- Neighborhood Gym:

  - "Become a Better You: Sign up for a free trial class and discover your inner strength."

- Community Bookstore:

  - "Uncover Hidden Treasures! Visit us this weekend for our book blind date event"

- Local Gardening Service:

  - "Love your yard again! Call today for a personalized gardening plan tailored to your yard."

Personas v General Targeting

Personas can be a helpful tool in your marketing arsenal, but you shouldn't ignore the value of broad brand awareness either. Getting too specific with your targeting might cause you to miss opportunities with people who are on the fringe of those targeting parameters. We will delve into this topic more in Risk #9.

The Customer Journey

The customer journey is exactly that. It's the journey your customer will take to become a loyal patron of your business. You may have heard of the term "sales funnel". A sales funnel is a visual representation of how your customers go from not knowing who you are to the point of sale. If you google 'sales funnel' (I don't recommend doing that without a free day and a lot of coffee), you will see that there are probably as many different variations of sales funnels as there are businesses. In general though, sales funnels can usually be broken down into these stages:

- Brand awareness

- Consideration

- Action

Naturally, the number of people in this funnel gets smaller in lower stages of the funnel. So, you want to make sure you have elements in place that are continually moving people through these stages. If you don't, then the customers you do get will come by sheer luck. As we explore the possible marketing risks you will need to take, we will identify which stage that risk will best apply to.

ONLINE TOUCH POINTS

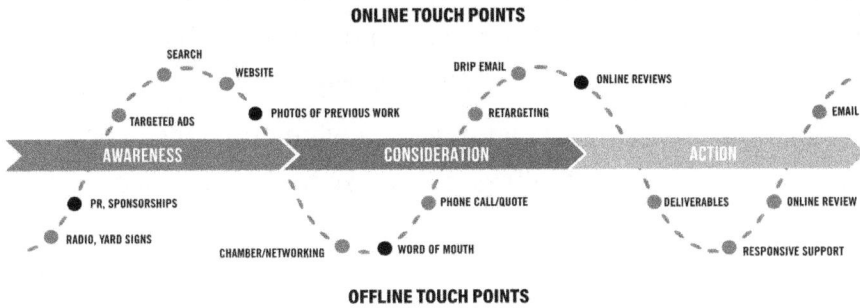

The diagram above depicts an example of how a typical customer might move through a sales funnel. You can see several touch points along this journey that nudge the customer from awareness to action.

Each touch point can help get from one stage to the next. Some touch points carry more weight than others. If you can imagine a scale for your potential customers that ranges from 0 to 10. 0 being that they've never heard of you and 10 is a loyal customer. The question that all marketing tries to answer is "how do I get my customers from 0 to 10 efficiently?". Some of these touch points might nudge a customer one number at a time. Some might leapfrog them down the journey. Think of customer journeys that you have been on yourself. What were the touch points that led you from 0 to 10? Consider two different scenarios:

In the first, your friend tells you about his recent date night with his spouse. They went to a restaurant that was familiar to you and then went to a new axe throwing arena. If you don't have one of these in your town, you might be wondering what kind of business this could be. Let me explain... Think of a bowling alley. But instead of a smooth wood floor with pins at the end, imagine a caged area with a target on a wooden wall. Now, instead of a bowling ball, you have (you guessed it) an axe!

As you can imagine, this is a unique experience and it made an impression on your friend. Until this point you probably have heard of it, maybe even saw a billboard for it, but that's about it. On our customer journey range, you were probably a 1 or 2. However, having a trusted friend that excitedly told you of his experience pushed you to a 6 or 7. In fact, the next week, when you and your spouse started the infinite Saturday night convo of "What do you want to do? I don't know, what do you want to do? I don't know, what do you want to do?" ad infinitum, you broke the cycle and said, "hey, Jerry told me about that new axe house. Want to give it a shot?" Having a trusted friend rave about a product carries a lot more weight than seeing that product in an ad.

In the second scenario, you're looking for a coat for hiking this winter. You are aware of several leading brands, and so you may already be at a 2 or 3 on the scale with some of them. You really like Patagonia and have bought one of their shirts before so technically you are already at a 9 with them, on the verge of becoming a repeat customer. You hate buying clothes online, so you head over to the local REI to see them in person. You find a particular style and material that you really like, but they don't have the color you want in your size. Disappointed, but determined you head home and jump on your computer to find the perfect winter hiking coat. After typing "patagonia coat" into Google, you see some ads for other brands that you've never heard of (you just went from 0 to 1 on this new brand's customer journey). Curiosity gets the best of you and you click (you just went from 1 to 2). After a few minutes of looking on this up and coming brand's website, you find a coat that is better than you could have imagined, and you're now squarely in their consideration stage. To make sure you're not getting scammed, you jump back over to Google and search for the new brand's name + "reviews" to see what others have said. To your delight it has nearly 5 stars on all the major review platforms. You hop back to the page you had saved with your soon to be new coat and click 'Add to Cart'. About a month later after you've already broken in your new coat, you get an email that has a coupon to the coat maker's site just in time for payday.

As a bonus, let's reconsider the first scenario. Imagine that the same events happened, but the timeline was different: your friend tells you about the axe throwing arena, then several weeks go by before you have a date night. So, a lot has happened to make you forget about your friend's story so you might not remember axe throwing as an option. However, if the axe arena was nudging you along that journey efficiently, they would more likely be a top of mind choice. Some ways they might have nudged you before and after your friend telling you about them are billboards, digital display ads, streaming radio commercials, and more. If the only nudge you got was from your friend, there is little chance you would be visiting the axe arena a month later.

The main takeaway here is that each customer is going to follow a slightly different path and there is not a silver bullet that will get them from 0 to 10 every time. Word of mouth is often touted as a supposed silver bullet. And while it does tend to be effective, we only know the times it works; we don't know how often it doesn't work. Consistent nudging along that journey is vital for your business's growth.

Understanding your target audience, and what types of marketing tactics connect with them and push them along this journey, will help you better evaluate the pitfalls and profits of the marketing risks we will cover throughout the book. The last element that you should know about your customers that will help you determine which marketing risks you want to take is your Customer Lifetime Value.

Customer Lifetime Value

Customer Lifetime Value, or CLV as we will call it, is a magic number that helps you determine how much you can spend on your marketing efforts. This number represents how much money your customers are actually making you. The formula below will help you determine, after all the costs are accounted for, how much green is coming to you. Without detailed tracking of how much individual customers are spending with you over time, how long you keep an average customer, and what your profit margins are, it will be very difficult to determine the CLV for your business. That's why keeping your data in some way is essential to your business's long-term growth.

To get a good idea of your CLV we will need to introduce you to a few other acronyms, namely, your CAC (customer acquisition cost) and your CTS (cost to serve). Your CAC is how much it costs for you to acquire a new customer. The lower this is, the better. Your CTS is how much it costs for you to not only serve that customer, but ideally this should also consider how much it costs to KEEP that customer. You can drive down the CTS with low quality products but you run the risk of losing those customers (and ultimately reducing your CLV). You should be able to get at least a rough idea of what your CTS is by examining the costs involved. If you're running a landscaping business, your CTS will include gas, labor, and equipment maintenance along with a portion of the software fees you use to send invoices and collect money, etc.

For now we are going to leave your CAC as undefined. By the end of this book you should be able to estimate what your CAC should be and how to keep it as low as possible.

Let's take a sneaker company for example. Their average customer stays with them for about 10 years and purchases a new pair of running shoes every year. If each pair of shoes costs $100, then over the course of that customer's relationship with the company, they will spend $1,000. If the cost to get those shoes to the customer costs about $50 (including manufacturing and distribution costs) then overall, if they spent no money on marketing and acquisition, they would have made about $500 over that customer's lifespan with you.

You can add your own numbers into this formula:

Y = average number of years a customer buys from you

A = average sale price

N = average number of sales per year

$$CLV = (Y \times A \times N) - CTS - CAC$$

For resources on how to keep track of your customer data along with some helpful tools, scan this QR code or visit theclimb.guide/clv.

I know, this looks like high school algebra all over again, but trust me, you owe it to yourself to understand this formula. (Y x A x N) gives you the total dollar amount that your average customer will give to you over their life as a customer. To get your

CLV (what a client is actually worth to you in dollars), you will need to subtract your CTS. If it didn't cost anything to get new customers then this number would be your CLV. Unfortunately, it's like the old saying goes, it takes money to make money, and in this case, it takes money to get a new customer. So, you have to subtract your CAC as well. However, we don't quite know what the CAC will be. Your CAC can be $1 or it could be $1000. As long as the final CLV is positive, you'll be making money. If your CLV is getting close to 0 or negative and you don't see your CAC getting lower, then you will want to rethink the cost of your products. Increasing how much you charge can increase your CLV, but only if the market can bear the increase.

As we go through this book we will keep CAC undefined, but keep in mind that in order to make money, your COA will always need to be less than your CLV. If your pre-COA CLV is $500, then you theoretically have $500 to acquire a new customer. As you can imagine, knowing this number can give you a lot of confidence in pursuing your marketing efforts if you can accurately track the COA.

Use this QR code to develop your SWOT analysis, goals, customer journey, and CLV online (theclimb.guide/plan).

Take some time to write down the details about your business that we've covered in this chapter. Having them in a form that you can reference will help you figure out which risks are right for you to take. Make sure you do this in pencil. As you write down your SWOT analysis, SMART Goals, Customer Journey, and CLV, you will begin to see that this needs to be an organic document. Your customer journey might influence what your opportunities are. Realizing your CLV might change the details of your goals.

Waking up, Eva wiped her mouth as she stretched in the vinyl chair. Luckily this one had the foot rest that she could extend. In her half-awake state, she could hear her dad and the physician joking about something. She wanted to close her eyes again, but then that sudden disoriented panic that you have when you wake up somewhere you are unfamiliar was like a bucket of cold water on her. She straightened herself up and brushed her hair from her face. The doctor, noticing her, said "Looks like someone could use some coffee. I'll have one of the nurses bring you a cup and let you two talk."

About that time there was a knock on the door, followed immediately by its opening (because no one ever waits for permission to enter a hospital room). Eva's brother, with wife and kids in tow, piled into the room. They had got up early to make the 3 hour drive from Charlotte, North Carolina. Hugs were exchanged, jokes about their father's age were made, and the grandkids bestowed upon him the crayola creations that they had made in the car ride to Burlington. Their dad reassured them that the doctor just wanted him to eat some oatmeal and go on a walk every day and he was going to be fine. When her brother tried to bring up the idea of retirement, her dad quickly shot it down. Eva's niece jumped into her lap and pulled out another card for her. It had what appeared to be the two of them on the front holding hands. She opened it up. "Happy Birthday Aunt Eva!". With the turbulence of the last 24 hours, she had forgotten that today was April 23rd, her 39th birthday.

A few days later Eva was helping her dad back into his house. He wasn't typically a fragile person, but his energy was low from the stay at the hospital. After she got his recliner ready for him and adjusted the temperature to be a little warmer, he said, "Eva, I've been thinking."

She didn't know what was going to come next, but felt like it deserved to be heard while sitting at the dining room table. "Have a seat Dad. I'll make us some tea."

As he eased himself into the seat, he said, "I've been thinking about the store. I can't remember what it's like to not run that business. It's pretty much all I've done for the last 40 years and it's woven into me." As she turned up the heat on the kettle, she was anticipating what her dad was about to tell her and getting excited to tell her brother the news that her dad had finally decided to sell! "And if I'm honest, I have to admit that not having the store is a little scary. But I think I've carried it as far as I can. I've barely broken even for the last few years, and I realized something while I was sitting in that god forsaken hospital. If I try to hang on to it, I'm either going to run it into the ground or myself, or both!"

She sat down across from him as the water was heating. His eyes were serious and tender. "I can help you wrap up the bookkeeping and put it on the market, Dad. You need to focus on your health."

"No, No," he responded firmly and resolute. "I'm not going to sell it. That store is our family legacy." There was an awkward silence before he continued. "I pretty much ruined your birthday. So, consider this a late birthday present," he said as he pulled something from his pocket. He took her hand and placed something hard and metallic in it.

She looked down and recognized the worn down keys of the shop. She looked back at him and began to object, but was interrupted. "I know you have a life and this was never part of your plans, but I know you have it in you to make that store great once again. Don't say yes or no right now. Take these keys and think about it." This was not how she imagined this conversation going. She had never considered this. At the most, she figured her brother would be the one he would tap to take over the store. About that time the kettle let out a high pitch scream... a much needed diversion.

As she lay in bed that night, Eva rolled the keys over and over in her hand as she considered this potential new direction for her life. She had gone the college route and got a job because, well, that's what you were supposed to do. She had never considered running her own business, being her own boss. The more she thought about it the faster her mind and heart raced. The big question was - could it work? Could she make it make money? She definitely didn't want it to just be scraping by. She needed a plan. So, she did what she was good at. She got out of bed and grabbed her laptop, a pad of paper, and a pen, then went to work.

The first thing she did was write out a SWOT analysis. Since she was tied so closely to the store she knew she'd have to put forth extra effort to be objective. The shop had some strengths that were obvious:

- Its long standing reputation in the community. There wasn't a year that had gone by without Marley's Books and Toys appearing on the backs of the elementary schools' tee ball team. Her dad was always a big sponsor of the town's toy drive every year at Christmas. He also had a fairly large list of past customers… did he also have their names and numbers (she couldn't fathom her dad collecting email addresses) in a spreadsheet? It was hard to say, but it would be a much stronger strength if he had.

- The shop was also in the middle of downtown so it got a lot of traffic. It was surprising how many people would pop into the charming shop on an average day. Most would come in, browse around, and leave. "Hmmm… there might be an opportunity there too," she thought to herself.

- The shop was also the area's only licensed retailer of the Shadow Stalkers line of collectible figurines and accessories. The series was based off a movie trilogy of the same name about a league of monster hunters and had a near cult following. Occasionally people would travel a few hours from Atlanta to see her dad's selection.

- One of the biggest strengths that Marley's had was that her father had purchased the building the shop was in early on and it was paid off.

Eva paused for a moment, admiring the list that represented the best of what her father had built. But she knew the harder work was still ahead. As obvious as its strengths were, so were the weaknesses of the shop:

- The website hadn't really been updated since the early 2000s. While it had a nice nostalgic feeling, it might be scaring away potential customers.

- Due to her dad's changing health needs over the last several years the shop hours had been reduced and there were less evening hours.

- When her dad first opened the shop, it was more common to see businesses pop up with the name of the store owner: Johnson's Locksmith Service, Steve White Insurance, J Hanley Plumbing, and of course Marley's Books and Toys. However, now, branding for these names was becoming harder and less distinct compared to newer brands like Geico, Pop-a-Lock, Roto Rooter, and even a canned water company called Liquid Death. Her dad never put much energy into the visual branding of the shop and you could tell.

She sat back against her pillow, tapping the pencil against the notepad as she tried to mentally dissect any other vulnerabilities the business had. She thought of a few more things that had a negative impact on the business, but they were outside of her control and fit more appropriately under Threats. Then it hit her:

- Selection and pricing. The shop definitely had a niche in brainy toys, but it needed something that could appeal to a wider audience. She wasn't 100% about the pricing without doing some research, but she had a hunch that her dad's pricing had gradually increased over the years to be noticeably different from competitors'.

Eva already had ideas formulating about how to take advantage of the shop's strengths and turn those weaknesses into opportunities and she was excited to get them down on paper.

Opportunities:

There were some obvious, easy to handle weaknesses that could open up opportunities for new business:

- The store hours were the easiest. She could handle keeping the shop open till 8 to provide more opportunity for customers to come.

- The website was another opportunity. Not only would it help potential customers convert and take the time to visit if the website communicated the store's value better, but there might also be an opportunity to offer some items for sale on the site directly.

- She was pretty sure there would be opportunities for pricing changes, and new product offerings, but she needed to do some research first.

- For the last 10 years, marketing technology had surpassed her father's ability to keep up with it. In that time, social media had exploded on the scene. At one point, one of the teenagers who helped with holiday wrapping had set up a Facebook page, but since then the posting had been inconsistent at best. There was a lot of opportunity to expand the shop's reach through social media and possibly email marketing as well.

The decision to take the shop was looking a little brighter once she considered the potential for its success. However, she hadn't analyzed the shop's threats yet.

Threats:

Competition is the first thing she thought to research when it came to threats. Were there any other toy shops or book stores in Burlington? She went to Google and searched 'toy stores Burlington, GA' first. The results had an upside and a downside.

The upside was that of the 7 businesses within Burlington that Google offered up, there wasn't one other toy store. That was a plus! She scribbled in 'no other toy stores' under strengths. However, Marley's Toys and Books was not in the top 3 local results, or the 'map pack' as it's called. Google had put Wal-Mart, Target, and even a toy store 45 minutes away above the shop's listing. She quickly wrote in 'Google ranking' under weaknesses. As she looked at her dad's Google Business Profile listing, she noticed it did not have any reviews. She added 'and reviews' to her previous entry. She did the same search for 'book store'. She found that there was another book store in town, but from the looks of its website it didn't appear to be a strong competitor. With both searches the usual online suspects popped up in ads. So she started her list:

- Amazon (for toys and books)
- Walmart and Target (for toys)
- Possibly the other bookstore in town

She had noticed that, like many downtowns across America, the amount of foot traffic had gradually declined. Back in the shop's prime her dad could bring in a few thousand dollars in one weekend just from the foot traffic through downtown. She had also noticed that a few of the shops that had been landmarks on main street had gone out of business and 'for lease' signs were hanging in the window. So she added:

- Declining downtown business

She knew that there were probably other things she could list in her SWOT analysis as she went along, but was happy with this first draft.

She decided to consider what some potential goals for the business could be. She knew enough about the life of the store to make some educated guesses about bills, costs of products, profit margins, and what resources could be leveraged to help it grow and came up with these SMART goals:

- See 15% increase in Shadow Stalker sales from last year.

- Increase daily in-store visitors by 20%

- See at least 10% of monthly sales from repeat customers by year's end.

She sat back and stared at the blueprints of a plan she had in front of her, wondering if she could make Marley's make money... wondering if it was worth the risk of her leaving her current, stable, good-paying job. She knew there were a lot of risks involved, but to her, this mountain was worth it.

The next day she drove to her dad's house with butterflies in her stomach. The kind you have before jumping off a tall rock into the water. She knocked on the door before opening it and found her dad in the kitchen making coffee. "Hey old man," she said as she set the groceries she had picked up for him on the counter. Oatmeal, turkey bacon, and skim milk. He picked up the turkey bacon and immediately regretted telling her about his new dietary restrictions before tossing it back on the counter with a sarcastic "Are you trying to kill me?"

He poured them both a cup of coffee as she put the groceries away. They sat down at the table. "Did you see on the news.." he started, but was interrupted by her.

"Dad... I'm in."

A smile broke out across his face and he said "I was hoping you'd say that! Stay right here. I have something for you." He went into the next room and returned with an envelope with her name on it. She opened it up to reveal a check for $10,000.

"Dad, I can't take this," she said as she tried to hand it back.

He held out his hand with a serious look on his face. "Eva, that old shop needs a lot of work. I couldn't live with myself if I gave you a lame horse and asked you to win a race on it. Take this and do whatever you need to do with it to make Marley's Toys and Books win that race. I cashed in a little of my retirement money. Just consider it a business loan. Pay me back as you are are able."

The next day was Monday. She went to work with a letter of resignation in hand and had a long conversation with her boss who pleaded with her to stay. She agreed to work for the next month as they found a replacement. She headed to the shop every day after work and began pouring over the records to see what information she could use. Her dad stayed with her to answer any questions she had. She knew she would have to put in extra hours to be ready to climb this mountain and face the risks ahead of her.

CHAPTER 2: THE RISK OF BRANDING

Risk: High
Reward: Long-term, high (possibly short term advantages too), distinction, notability, makes all other tactics more efficient.
Customer Journey: Applies to all stages

"Marley's Toys and Books". Eva Marley had become so familiar with the name of the shop, she had never questioned whether it was a good name until her SWOT analysis. The idea of changing it bothered her -she didn't like the idea of taking her family name off the business, but she knew that if the branding was holding the business back, the sooner it could be changed the better. For the last week she had rolled around different names in her head. Nothing seemed to stick. She thought about her target audiences. There were the young kids (and their parents) who loved the tactile puzzle toys and blocks, the hipster parents who all but refused to buy their kids phones or tablets - they loved the thought provoking games, science kits, and outdoor toys that were in the shop, and then there was the crowd that came solely for the rare books and Shadow Stalkers. Then it dawned on her -- Staci, a graphic designer at her work fit 2 of those categories. She had even visited the shop for the last two Christmases to get her daughter gifts. The next day Eva went directly to Staci's desk. "Hey Staci, do you do freelance work?"

"Sure, if it's cool enough or pays enough."

"Well, I hope this is really cool because I don't have a lot to pay you. I need a new name and logo for my da... for my shop. Can you help? I have $500 I can use for this."

With a smile, Staci said, "I'm in. Let's talk about the details over a margarita this afternoon!"

Think of your favorite shoes. Can you picture the logo of the brand? What do you think about when you think of those shoes? Their quality, comfort, durability, aesthetic? Do you remember the last ad or commercial you saw for that brand? The experience you've had with those shoes and that company are all things that inform your perception of that company's brand.

Your customers have analogous experiences of your brand as well. What do they envision? How does it make them feel?

Your brand is the foundation, not only of your marketing, but of your business itself. Protect it and your business will thrive. Neglect it at your own peril. If you are starting a business, then you have one of the biggest decisions to make that will affect your marketing and therefore your success for the life of your business: **the name of your brand**.

There have been various trends in business naming. At one point names like AAA, or ABC were very common because they got first placement in the phone book. You've probably seen one of these branding dinosaurs in your town. Another common practice has been to name the business after the founder, as in "Andrews Insurance" or "Russell's Chevrolet." While this practice is still more prevalent than the alphabetical algorithm approach, it is phasing out.

Some new businesses can survive a restrictive name like that, but for many it can deal a death blow to the marketing. Older brands that became household names in the mid 1900's have transcended the constraints of their founder-referencing monikers. McDonalds, Harley Davidson, and Wal-Mart are all examples of businesses named after founders that have been wildly successful. However, it's harder to imagine a business named this way to start and rise to national acclaim today. Times have changed, and what people expect out of large brands has changed as well. There is a reason why Facebook wasn't called Zuckerburg's Social Media Company. Your business name either helps or hurts all the marketing that comes after it.

For some businesses, naming the business after the founder's last name doesn't hurt, but outside of having a very unique name, I would posit that it doesn't help any businesses in the long run either. However, there are exceptions to this rule. If your name fits the overall brand, then it might work. For instance, if you started a country diner and your name was Gracie calling the restaurant Gracie's Diner or Gracie's Kitchen could work. The 'feeling' of the name lends itself to a place that serves chicken fried chicken, mashed potatoes, and gravy. However, if your name happened to be Joshua, then you might consider a different naming strategy, because Josh's Diner just doesn't have the same charisma that Gracie's does. Another thing to consider when you name your business is whether or not that name can be as effective in a new town as it is in the current one. If it can't, then you are limiting your growth potential at the start. If you put your town's name in your business name, then you are limiting yourself geographically. If you decide to open another shop in a neighboring county in the future, you're most likely going to have to rebrand. Better to start off right instead of investing time and money into a brand that might ultimately change. Naming a business in these ways feels safe, but as we have seen, it runs the risk of limiting growth.

Creating a name that stands out feels scary. It's an unknown world to many. Will people like it or hate it? There is no guarantee. Whenever you consider a business name that is somewhat out of the norm, you will want to examine it from several angles (can it easily be used in a joke, is it hard to pronounce, etc.), but naming your business something that can draw attention and scale with you is a risk worth taking. Can you imagine if Alphabet founders Larry Page and Sergey Brin had named Google after themselves? "Page Brin Search Services" or perhaps, the more clever "Search Bringine". It's hard to imagine either of those names making it in a modern world. Our culture has come to recognize certain naming signals that convey quality and credibility. Going against those limits your ability to scale, or at best makes it much harder.

With many of the tactics we will explore in this book, there are risks associated with both using them and with not using them. The hard part is choosing which of those risks is worth taking. However, branding exemplifies this duality more than all the others. Having a distinct brand seems risky, but having an indistinct brand is terminal.

Pros and cons of rebranding

It's important to note that every business is unique and there is not a one-size fits all approach to branding -- the history of your brand in the community, the future goals of the business, and the current resources you can devote to a rebranding project. If the business name has 25 years of history in the community, and the goal is to sell in 3 years, then rebranding might be a poor choice. However, if revenue has been slipping and the business needs a boost, then rebranding might give it the injection of energy that it needs to carry through and increase its valuation for a future sale. Either way, there are some known pros and cons to rebranding that are important to consider:

Cons:

- Losing the name recognition of the old brand. If your business is well-known, rebranding might cause a dip in brand awareness as the community at large and even loyal customers get used to the new brand. However, if you do it right, with good PR and communication to your customers, this dip can be minimized.

- The cost of rebranding collateral. If your business is 5-10 years old or older, then you probably have branded material that is lingering around that will need to be tossed. This is anything from business cards to car wraps. When you rebrand, it's usually best to rip the bandaid off. This may be a good time to evaluate what printed material is really beneficial for your business. You will also need to rebrand your digital assets such as your website and social media profiles. As you can imagine, the price tag on a rebrand can get pretty high, pretty fast.

Pros:

- Rebranding injects new energy into your business and gives you the opportunity to make a bit of a splash and catch people's attention in a way that you haven't before.

- It allows you to clarify the mission and messaging of the business so that the new brand clearly represents the personality and vision of your organization.

- If your current brand isn't getting the job done, rebranding can help reverse the decaying momentum of a brand that has lost impact and relevance. If the brand is still young, but was developed poorly, then rebranding can save the business before a bad brand takes it under.

- Longevity and Scalability. Moving from a weak brand to a strong brand will help ensure the longevity of the business. If the old brand was restrictive, then a new brand can help set the stage for easier scalability and growth.

If a bad brand makes it, it's out of sheer luck and determination. Don't leave your business in the hands of luck. Work smarter by investing in the development of a great brand.

Your brand is more than just your name and logo. From your customers' perspective, your business has one identity. It's how they feel about your product or service. It's what they think of when they see your logo. On the other side, you know your business inside and out. You know its strengths and weaknesses. Part of your brand is made of that as well as the vision of what you want it to be. The third element of your brand is how you communicate that vision to the world. These are things like your logo, your messaging, anything visual or audible that your business puts out to the world with its name on it. Your brand lives in a dynamic space where these three things overlap. You can control two elements of your brand, but part of your brand will live with your customers. So treat them well.

A lot of ink has been spilled in marketing textbooks about differentiation. We have taken it as a natural law that you must differentiate yourself from your competition. You have to have an 'angle'. You have to be better at something, cheaper, higher quality, faster, more horsepower, etc. However, differentiation only matters after you've caught the attention of your audience. Your audience doesn't want to see a bullet point list of why they should choose you. You have to reach them on a gut level before they ever care to read your bullet pointed list. Your brand has to capture their heart before you get a chance to speak to their mind (more on this in Risk #9). Because the truth is, your competition will always do something better, but they can't do your brand better than you. Be bold, stand out.

In his pioneering work, *How Brands Grow*, Byron Sharp emphasizes the concept of distinction over differentiation in brand strategy. Sharp challenges the traditional marketing belief that successful branding is about differentiating products from competitors. Instead, he argues that one key to growth is brand distinctiveness, ensuring that consumers easily recognize and remember the brand. When your brand is easy to spot in a crowd, it helps your customers build a relationship with it. The better someone can look out across their options and spot your brand, the easier it is for them to build memory structures around it, so that when they are ready to buy, the other brands fade into a blur and yours stands out.

Sharp points out that most markets are saturated with similar products, making true differentiation rare and often irrelevant to consumers. He suggests that what really matters is not how different a product is, but how easily it can be noticed and recalled by consumers. This is where brand distinctiveness comes into play. It involves creating and using unique brand assets like logos, colors, slogans, and packaging styles that stand out in the consumers' minds.

Brand Words:

- Distinctiveness:
  - Memorable
  - Recognizable
  - Standout
  - Unique
  - Iconic
  - Salient
  - Striking
  - Notable
  - Bold
  - Unmistakable
- Differentiation
  - Innovative

- ○ Superior

- ○ Advanced

- ○ Customized

- ○ Niche

- ○ Exclusive

- ○ Premium

- ○ Specialized

- ○ Pioneering

- ○ Unparalleled

PITFALL WARNING:

Don't ask people what they think about your logo (or any other design). The problem with getting feedback this way is that if you ask them to think, they will do just that. And unfortunately, most people won't be thinking about your branding when they are making buying decisions. Look at all the logos that are around you -- on your shoes, on your phone, in your car. When is the last time you really stopped and thought about them? Instead of asking people what they think about your design, ask them specific questions that give you insight into whether or not it aligns with your brand, like "does this design look credible to you?" or "does this logo feel fun?" The end goal is to understand what sort of feeling and gut reaction your design evokes without having people think too much about it. More on this later in chapter 10, "Marketing to Humans."

That afternoon Eva and Staci went to a Mexican restaurant down the street from their office called Cancun's. The jumbo margarita was half price and they took advantage of the bargain. Eva explained to Staci that she felt like the name of the shop and the traditional looking logo didn't do the business justice. It needed something, and if there was any way to keep Marley in the name and make it distinctive then she would lean towards that. Staci was up for the challenge and said that naming a business is one of the most important things for a business's success. The name and branding lay the foundation for everything else. She asked Eva, "What are some adjectives that describe Marley's Toys and Books?" They started writing words down on a napkin:

- Fun

- Whimsical

- Magical

- Brainy

- Nerdy

- Gifts

- Rare

- Old Books

They looked at the list and pulled out their phones to consult an online thesaurus. They paired words together like Magical Marley's, and Marley's Whimsical Gifts, and even tried to create new words. Then Staci said, "It's almost like the shop is an orphanage for lost books and really cool toys, just waiting to be matched with a good home." Slurping up the last of her frozen drink she laughed, "Marley's home for toys and books".

Eva sat up and said, "Yes! That's it. But it needs something else... They aren't just any books and toys. How about Marley's Home for Wayward Books and Gifted Toys?"

"Holy shit!" Staci exclaimed, "it's like something out of Harry Potter. I would go there all the time!"

Eva sat back, proud of her stroke of naming genius. It could still be called "Marley's" for short and the longer name would be intriguing enough to hook in her target audience. She knew that a great brand would increase the effectiveness of all the other marketing elements. It would also directly help achieve goal #2.

CHAPTER 3: THE RISK OF OUTSOURCING

Risk: Medium to High
Reward: Medium to High (possibly short term advantages too), distinction, notability, makes all other tactics more efficient.
Customer Journey: Applies to all stages

The next evening when Eva was at the shop reviewing the shop's monthly bills, she asked her dad, "What is this bill you pay $400 for every month to WebCorp Inc?"

"Oh, that's my digital marketing. They make my website and make sure that my ad is in the telephone directory."

"How long have you been paying them that much?" Eva asked.

"Oh, they probably called here about 4 years ago. I figured it would be easier to just pay them to do it than to figure it out on my own."

Eva was trying to contain her burning rage that some sketchy corporation would charge her dad $4800 year after year for a dumpy website that was barely findable on Google and an ad in the phone book of all places. "Dad, we need to cancel this immediately. How many of your customers do you think even know what a phone book is?"

At Epic Nine, we've heard countless clients tell us stories of being scammed by local and national marketing companies. We even had one client who had been paying her previous web designer yearly for her domain name. When she informed him that she was switching services, he tried to hold her domain name up for a $1,000 ransom. Working with an agency can either be the best or worst thing for your business. That's why being able to speak the marketing language and knowing how to evaluate your marketing's effectiveness is vital to you not getting scammed. Here are some things to consider when thinking about hiring an agency:

- Are they local or national?
  - There is something attractive about going with a national brand. It feels like it makes sense. They've "helped thousands of other businesses just like you!" right? Well, maybe. They may have set up a lot of websites for businesses just like yours or even run social media accounts for businesses like yours. But that doesn't necessarily mean they've helped them. One of the most common stories we hear about the frustrations of working with a national brand is that

they will post generic content on social media accounts and their websites all look the same. This happens a lot with national marketing agencies that target specific niches. For instance, a "dental office marketing company" might give the same website and social media content for a dentist in your town as they do for one or more in the next town over. We see this with dental, medical, home services, legal, and more. They also don't know your local target audience as well as a local company would. That's not to say that all local marketing or design companies are great, but I believe that most of them are as good or better of an option for your business than becoming just another small business client for a large national corporation.

- How many people are on their team?

  o Many times a local company might not be an actual company in the technical sense, but rather, a freelancer. Freelancers aren't necessarily bad. I was a freelancer for a few years before starting Epic Nine, and my wife has been a freelancer for over 20 years. You can find great talent at an affordable price with freelancers, but if your marketing is fast paced, and if you want to build a long-standing relationship with a stable designer then expect to pay more. The college student with a graphic design side hustle might not be around after graduation. That's not to say that many design students haven't established long successful freelancing careers. They have. But it's important to consider the risks if you are going to outsource this vital part of your business. Companies that have a 3+ team members can usually provide great work at an affordable price with decent support. However, always check Google and social media reviews to see how other businesses rate them. Consider how long they have been in business. What has the evolution of their company looked like? Will you be working with the same person through your whole relationship with them? All of these are important factors when picking a designer or agency to work with.

- What does success look like?

  o One of the most important things to clarify with the person or agency you are hiring is what success looks like. One of the situations we have seen time and time again is a lack of metric-awareness from business owners. If business is going well they tend to not ask any questions about KPIs or ROI and assume that all the parts of their business are working like a well oiled machine. However, the minute traffic to the store starts to dip, then all eyes turn towards the marketing agency or consultant. The rational thing to ask in this case is, how are you measuring success? If you are paying for something, how do you know you are getting what you are paying for? If you haven't set (and agreed on) some clear goals with your marketing agency, designer, or consultant, then it's hard to hold their feet to the fire if things go south. You may have asked for a website, they might not have known you meant you wanted to sell 20 more washers a month. If goals are discussed and agreed on, then both parties will have more interest in measuring them as well.

- Do they bring fresh ideas?

  o Great marketing involves more than just the technical aspects of design, social media, and advertising. It requires creative insight. Rory Sutherland wisely puts it this way, "The power of a good idea or an insight is that it can save you a fortune. It is very cheap leverage." In this light, creativity is not just an artistic endeavor; it's a strategic tool that can yield significant returns on investment.

- o Creative marketing does more than just sell a product; it creates an experience, evokes emotions, and builds lasting relationships with the audience. It turns the mundane into something remarkable, fostering a deeper connection between the brand and its customers. Sutherland notes, "Logic and facts need to be supplemented with something more engaging."

- o In a world where consumers are bombarded with endless streams of content, the ability to stand out is more important than ever. A marketing agency that can think outside the box, challenge norms, and bring fresh, innovative ideas to the table is an invaluable asset. As the advertising pioneer David Ogilvy put it, "You cannot bore people into buying your product; you can only interest them in buying it."

Another thing to solidify when you first hire someone is what exactly you are paying for. For the first few years after starting Epic Nine, I made the poor assumption that our clients knew more than they did. After living in the digital marketing world for so long, I just took certain things as common knowledge because it was a part of my daily life.

People in every industry tend to do this to some extent or another. You might have a medical professional in your family that uses acronyms and words like contusion (bruise) or edema (swelling) in regular conversation as if we all had a medical degree, or the gearhead that will tell you exactly what's going in your car's engine to make that weird noise you've been hearing and expect you to follow along. This is a cognitive bias called "the curse of knowledge". It occurs when someone who is knowledgeable about a specific subject finds it difficult to think about the subject from the perspective of someone who is less informed. This bias can lead to a communication gap, where the well-informed individual assumes that others have the background to understand what is being discussed as clearly as they do.

In essence, once you know something, it's hard for you to imagine what it's like to not know it. The reason this is relevant for your marketing journey is because you need to be aware of it so that you know what questions to ask, but also to understand that you are the authority on your business and you shouldn't expect someone who helps you with marketing to know all the nuances of what you do.

To help you do this, ask for a clear outline of the scope of work you are hiring someone for. This will save you both frustration in the long run. A scope of work might answer questions like:

- How many pages will the website contain?

- How many versions and revisions of a design are included?

- How many hours are included?

- How many social media posts are included?

- How much time for strategy and reporting is included each month?

- Is SEO included?

- Will the website be ADA compliant?

You will also want the deliverables clearly defined in your marketing agreement. The deliverables are the things that you will actually get at the end of the project. If you are building a website, knowing who owns the website is important. Also, receiving all relevant files for your branding can save you a lot of headaches in the future (more on that soon).

The next day Eva called WebCorp and spoke with their customer service rep. She insisted that they cancel the account. Her dad had just paid for the month in advance, so she had one month to figure out what to do about a new website. She knew she didn't have the time to do it, but she also knew that whoever she hired to do it needed to be local, reliable, able to track things on the website and affordable. The good news is that her marketing budget for the year just got an extra $400 a month!

She didn't know how to begin finding a new company to design the website. She had dealt with marketing firms in her role at the hospital, but she knew their fees were way outside of what she could afford. So she texted Staci, "Do you know of any good web designers around Burlington?" Staci wasn't a web designer herself, but she knew what to look for.

Staci shot back, "Web Monkeys - crazy name, serious websites. They know their stuff and do a lot more than websites, so they know how to make all your marketing work together. Plus, they are super cool over there."

Eva googled "Web Monkeys Burlington". Their Google Business Profile listing had several 5 star reviews from other business people she was familiar with. She clicked on their site and went immediately to their portfolio page. The websites they listed as their recent work all looked unique and custom to the brand of the business they were designing them for. For good measure, Eva visited a few other companies in the Burlington area as well to see what they offered, but their sites and portfolio didn't seem to match up to what Web Monkeys had.

CHAPTER 3: THE RISK OF OUTSOURCING

CHAPTER 4: THE WEBSITE MOUNTAIN

Priority: High
Customer Journey: Every stage

Eva woke up early on the last week of her old job to get a head start on some things she had to have finished. At the top of the list was the website. Marleystoysandbooks. com was nothing short of a disaster. The hours were wrong, the images were old, and the logo was pixelated. Perhaps Web Monkeys could help, but she needed some ideas first. She figured that some other book or toy store out there had a good looking website so she began searching in larger cities for someone who was doing it right to give her some inspiration. Most were not much better, but she was able to find a few that had a great brand and they carried it through all the elements of their site. She saved them to her bookmarks and headed to work.

That day, she met Staci for lunch to review the logos she had created. After placing their order at the counter, they took the metal stand with their order number, printed on a small laminated cardstock and wedged in between the two metal circles at the top and found an empty booth near a window. Staci slid across the worn vinyl seat before unlatching her laptop bag and pulling out a sticker-covered MacBook. "I can't wait for you to see these!" she said, as she fired up the old but trusty computer. Once the screen came to life and she switched to the right app, she spun the computer around on the table and anxiously asked, "Whatdoya think?".

It was perfect. Staci had taken the ideas they had brainstormed while naming: magical, rare, fun, etc. and built the logo to evoke those feelings. When Eva saw it, she made a high pitched shriek of excitement. "OMG Staci! You did it! You gave Marley's a new face!"

Staci's face lit up with the approval, "Yay! Now, I'll get you some business cards and tags mocked up and send over all the files you'll need to get things printed."

Looking Under the Hood:

The Technical Aspects of Your Designs

File Types

Whenever you have something designed, there can be several types of files that you might get. For print design and branding, it's pretty straightforward. Below are a list of the different file types you will need to understand:

- PDF: This is a pretty standard document file that can usually be sent directly to a printer to be printed. Many times, proofs of designs will come in a PDF or JPG format.

- PNG: PNGs are typically only used for web. The main benefit that a png file has is that it can have a transparent background. Any time you are sending your logo to be used online, you will want to send a png version so your logo isn't the one with an ugly white background around it. You typically don't want to send photos as pngs because the file size will be unnecessarily large.

- JPG: JPG (or JPEG) files are typically the best format to send and receive photos. They can also be used to send proofs or mockups, but should be avoided for print. When you are sending photos for a design, you can often tell when the file will be usable by its size. If it's 500KB or less, then it's probably not a great file size for printing. However, 250K and up can possibly be used on websites.

- EPS: EPS files are a core file that you want for your logo and branding files. This is a format that can be used at any size of print and remain high quality. Final logo files should be requested in EPS format. If you are working with your printer directly, the eps or pdf files will be preferred.

- AI: AI stands for Adobe Illustrator. These are considered the working files of a design. You will rarely need them, but they are helpful to have in case you work with multiple designers. Without an understanding of Illustrator, these files can be difficult to work with.

- PSD and INDD: These are associated with the Adobe programs, Photoshop and InDesign respectively. You will typically not need these, but it's good to know what they are in case you are working with more than one designer and they need files from each other.

If you already have logo files that you will be sending to a designer to use, you will be their best friend if you can send it to them in EPS, AI, or PDF format. That is because these formats are usually vector files (as opposed to bitmaps) which means they can be scaled up or down without degrading the quality. If you only have a smaller jpg or png file, then it can be a good investment to have a designer convert that logo into a vector format.

Website Platforms

For websites, the files and technology involved are a little more complex. The core of any website will typically involve HTML, CSS, and Javascript. If you are lucky, you will never have to deal directly with any of these. If you have any sort of content management system, or CMS, then you might also have a database. Typically, you will not need direct access to your files or database, but if you request them, make sure you or someone you are working with knows what to do with them. Most websites today utilize some sort of CMS platform to generate those your website and use a whole other level of programming to do so.

Wordpress is the most popular CMS technology to date. It has been around for over 20 years and powers sites that range from a basic blog to multinational ecommerce brands. Shopify is also a popular choice for ecommerce sites. Others include Wix, Webflow, Weebly (programmers must love W names!), GoDaddy Website Builder, and Squarespace.

The main difference between Wordpress and most other platforms is that you can customize it to do whatever you need it to do and look any way you need it to look. Platforms that don't allow for this sort of customization by their nature limit how well your brand can be implemented on them. With Shopify, Wix, Webflow, and the others, you are limited to hosting your website with them. With Wordpress sites, you have the ability to scale your site's hosting needs up or down depending on your needs. Where and how your site is hosted can affect its security, how fast it loads, and its uptime. You can expect to pay $25 or more for good, reliable hosting with good support. The cost can vary based on the level of performance and/or service.

For services such as Wix, Webflow, or GoDaddy, you can't get access to the files, but you might request admin or ownership of the account with which they are associated.

Having a basic understanding of file types and their associated technology can help reduce a lot of back and forth on emails ("Thanks, but I need the vector files.") and frustration involved with communication around these things. Understanding what you need and should have will also help protect your business in case you ever have to part ways with a marketing or design partner.

When the server brought their food, Eva took the opportunity to switch the conversation to the website. She felt like this was going to be a lengthy, expensive process and didn't want to get in over her head. "Can you tell me about websites? I want to get this right. Have you ever designed one before?" She asked.

Staci chuckled and said, "Well, at least you are approaching it with some humility. A lot of people think anyone can build a website - their teenage nephew, a college intern, themselves."

Eva explained that she had helped build her dad's first website as part of a group project in college, and quickly made it clear that it was her first and last website design venture.

"Well, I don't do websites either," Staci said. "It's just not my thing. To really be able to design a website well you need to be able to understand some of the underlying code and how it's built." Staci continued, "However, my previous gig was with a small marketing agency in my hometown. I got to see how the process works. I can tell you a couple of pointers to help you get a kick-ass site." Eva grabbed her phone and opened up the notes app to jot down the pointers. In between bites Staci laid out a framework for the design process:

- Know what success looks like. Don't tell them that "you'll know it when you see it". Designers of all stripes hate that. Have a good idea of what you want your site to look like and how it needs to function. Examples are great.

- When you give them revisions make sure you are as thorough as possible. Be brutal if you have to be. Just remember that if it doesn't look like what you want it to, it might not be the designers fault completely. You might not be effectively articulating what you want. Designers have lots of superpowers, but mind reading isn't one. If your first thought is that you want it to "pop", then think of a more specific way to describe what you are looking for. Oftentimes people will use vague words like 'pop' or 'stand out', because they can't articulate what they are looking for. "Pop" means something different to everyone, so taking the time to formulate specifics of what you are looking for can save everyone's sanity. One option is to find designs that are similar to the style you are looking for.

- Understand that once you approve a design, it's really a pain to go back and change it, especially if they have already started building it out as a website.

- Knowing what you want it to look like is one thing, knowing what you want it to do is another. Make sure you tell them on the front end everything you need it to do... Do you want to sell things, have a calendar of events, a blog, or a chat feature? Get those on the front end, so they can work it into your quote.

Eva put down her phone and pondered this process, giving Staci a chance to tend to her neglected lunch.

"So.... How much does a good website cost?"

"Somewhere between $1,000 and $100,000." Staci replied sarcastically, laughing to herself. Eva looked confused. Staci realized that she didn't get the joke. "It's really hard to say. In some ways, it's like art. You can find a gorgeous painting at a craft fair for $100 or you can go pay someone a million dollars for a painting that required no more skill to paint than the craft fair painting, but they can charge more simply because they are a famous painter."

Eva started to understand. Staci continued, "If you went to 5 different agencies in our region, you'd probably get 5 different prices for nearly the same quality of site." What I've seen is that you might get a great website closer to the $1000 range, but it's a crap shoot. You have an equal chance of getting a horrible one."

On the other hand, you're almost guaranteed a great website for $30,000, but is it really worth the price?"

"I'd be broke before I started!" Eva laughed.

"I think, if you aimed for the $5,000 mark, and went with a company that has a proven track record, you'd be safe. Remember, this isn't something you want to leave up to chance. Your website is going to be the cornerstone to all your other marketing. It will cost you time and money in the long run if you slack on it in the beginning."

They finished their lunch and talked about some of the possible changes Eva was going to make to the shop. As they were getting ready to leave, Staci said, "Oh, and all of that stuff I told you about the web design process, it applies to graphic design in general. You just got lucky with having a brilliant artist like me as a friend. Hang on to that logo, because it might be worth a million dollars one day." Eva responded, "Well, in that case, let me get the check."

That night, at the shop, Eva thought about their conversation. She could use some of the money her dad had given her for the website. It was definitely one of the things that needed improvement. She also thought about what it needed to do. She liked the idea of ecommerce, but she wondered if it was futile to try to compete with Amazon and other big box online retailers. Would people actually buy things from her online? If she was going to invest in selling online, she needed an angle, something her customers couldn't find cheaper somewhere else. She packed up her things at the shop. She was anxious to get answers to these questions and more at her meeting with Web Monkeys tomorrow.

For most local businesses, your website will be the cornerstone of your marketing. Potential customers will either search for your product or service and find it, click on a social media link and get there, manually type it in after seeing your print ad, or possibly search for you by name after they hear your ad on the radio. No matter how they get there, your website will either make all your marketing more or less effective. I've found it helpful to look at your website from 3 different viewpoints: 1) an aesthetic viewpoint, 2) a technical viewpoint, and 3) a practical viewpoint, considering how easy or hard it is for your web visitor to use.

Aesthetic:

The Aesthetic side is the one we typically think about when we think of web design. "How does it look?" Having a site that looks great is part of telling your story well. You get just a few seconds to convince your customers that they should choose you. Various studies have shown that a user will judge a website within the first few seconds of viewing it. Your site should easily make an impression on them. One study that evaluated what influenced trust or mistrust of medical websites (a category one might assume would be influenced by the content of the page rather than the design) found that 94% of the critics was design related and focused on things such as:

- Complexity

- Busy layout

- Lack of navigation aids

- Boring web design

- Use of color

- Pop-up adverts

- Slow introductions to the site

- Small print

- Too much text

- Corporate look and feel

- Poor search capabilities

only 6% was content related.

Great design attracts people to your business and instills trust. Poor design builds mistrust and hurts credibility.

For more information about user experience and ADA accessibility scan this QR code or visit theclimb.guide/ux

Technical:

Consider this: 93% of consumers have left a site when it did not load fast enough (YOTTA 2019). The more our technology advances, the faster people will expect websites to be. This is especially important with mobile devices. Most of your website traffic will be coming from mobile devices and since cellular data continues to be inconsistent in speed, your website should be optimized to load quickly no matter how fast a user's connection is. There are obvious extremes to this that can't be accounted for. And speaking of mobile devices, there is no reason that your website should not be responsive.

A website being responsive simply means that it responds to the size of the screen. As the screen size decreases from a desktop monitor to a mobile phone, the website should rearrange the content so that it remains legible and easy to navigate without having to zoom in to see text or scroll sideways for content.

Practical:

If your website design is phenomenal and it loads fast, then you are halfway to having the perfect site for your brand. The other half involves the overall experience the user has when they are on the site. While there is no standard for user experience, you should ask some of the following questions to help guide the process to help you walk away with a site that helps convert your website visitors into customers:

- Is the navigation intuitive and simple?

  o Can users easily find what they are looking for?
  o Is the menu structure straightforward and logical?

- Is the content clear and engaging?

  o Does the content effectively communicate the business's message?
  o Is the text easy to read, and are visuals appealing and relevant?

- Is the website accessible to all users?

  - Does it meet accessibility standards for users with disabilities (e.g., screen reader compatibility, keyboard navigation)?
  - Are color contrasts sufficient for easy reading?

- Is there a clear call to action?

  - Are calls to action (CTAs) prominent and clear?
  - Do CTAs guide the user to the next steps (e.g., purchase, sign-up, contact)?

- Is the website trustworthy and secure?

  - Is there an SSL certificate installed for secure browsing?
  - Are privacy policy, terms of service, and contact information easily accessible?

- Is the website optimized for search engines?

  - Are SEO best practices in place (keywords, meta tags, alt text for images)?
  - Is the site structure optimized for search engine crawling?

- How is the overall user experience?

  - Are there any frustrating aspects or barriers for users?
  - Is the overall aesthetic pleasing and aligned with the brand?

- Is there a feedback mechanism for users?

  - Is there an easy way for users to provide feedback about their experience?
  - Are there analytics in place to track user behavior and identify pain points?

Luckily the Web Monkeys' office was walking distance from the shop. Eva flipped the sign on the door to read 'out for lunch', locked up, and was on her way to tackle another marketing mountain. She spotted the sign with a monkey hanging off the end and thought to herself, well, at least they know how to do their own branding.

"You must be Eva," one of the designers greeted her, with her hand outheld.

"I am. I am here to talk with someone about my website," she said as they shook hands.

"Great! Let's meet in the conference room," she said as she led the way. "I'm Chloe, I will be the one helping program the website for you and doing all the nerdy back end stuff. I will get Ethan, he'll be the one crafting the look and feel of your website"

She left Eva in the modest Web Monkeys' conference room and returned quickly with Ethan. "Hi, I'm Ethan," he said as they shook hands.

"Nice to meet you," she replied.

"I love your new logo. We were all excited when we saw the change on your Facebook page!"

"Thanks! My friend Staci, who designed it, actually recommended you all."

"Well, tell her that we take that as a huge compliment coming from someone with her skills."

"So, you've probably already seen my current site, don't judge me."

Ethan laughed before reassuring her, "Don't worry. It's not the worst we've seen, but it definitely needs some help."

"If by help, you mean completely torn down and rebuilt, then yes."

"That was actually going to be our recommendation," Ethan chuckled. "I am glad we are on the same page!" Ethan continued, "A lot of the time, when people start working on their website they are thinking primarily about the question 'what does it need to look like?', but we like to start with the question 'what does it need to do for you?'" Eva nodded at this distinction she had never thought of before. "We like to start with your goals. At the end of the day, we aren't just asking 'what does a good website look like?' but 'what does a successful website look like?' So, what are your goals?"

Eva was surprised by the question. She hadn't expected to talk about goals with the website design, but it made total sense. Why wouldn't her website be designed and built to help her achieve those goals? She recited the goals to Chloe and Ethan:

- See 15% increase in (super cool product) sales from last year.

- Increase daily in-store visitors by 20%

- See at least 10% of monthly sales from repeat customers by year's end.

They looked slightly impressed. Ethan confided, "Most of our clients aren't able to answer that question. We usually have to help them figure out what their goals are. It's refreshing to have someone in here that can articulate their goals!"

Eva confessed, "Well, I should tell you that my previous career was in marketing, so I am familiar with some of this, but I never had to do too much with the web department."

Ethan jotted down the goals and they began looking over the list. "I believe the website can help with all of these goals, it's just a matter of figuring out how. The way I like to break it down is that there are two sides of this coin. One is having a great website. When people get to your site you have a few seconds to make an emotional connection with them. If it doesn't, then you aren't giving them a lot of reason to take the next step and come to your store. But the other side of this coin is getting people to your site. You can have a million dollar site, but if no one is coming to it, then you just wasted a million dollars!" Eva scrunched her nose at the thought of wasting any money on an ineffective website.

Ethan continued, "So, part of that seeing increased store visits and sales is seeing increased web visits. Part of getting more visits is your advertising. We can talk about that later, but another part is your search engine rankings. We never guarantee organic search engine rankings, and anyone who does is trying to con you. But we can give you the best tools to help you get there. We will want to make sure the right keywords are present on your site. Some of the things people should find you for are obvious, like 'toy stores burlington', but are there any searches that might not be obvious to us that you could potentially get some new customers from? Are there any toys or things that you sell that people would be searching for specifically?"

Eva thought, and then excitedly said, "Oh, we carry the Shadow Stalkers! We are the only regionally licensed seller of them. Sometimes, we have people come from Atlanta to get them."

Ethan looked intrigued. "Do you think they would buy them online if they had the opportunity?"

Eva responded, "Oh, I am sure they would! Most of the time, they are younger, so I am sure they are used to buying everything online."

Chloe jumped in and said, "Have you thought about an ecommerce site?"

"Sure, but I am not sure if it's worth it at this point. I am guessing that that probably costs a lot to get set up."

"You'd be surprised," assured Ethan. "But that is a good question to ask. Many people think 'if they build it, customers will come' with their ecommerce site, so it's good to really evaluate whether or not you'd make money with it."

Chloe, more familiar with the backend of ecommerce sites and all the configuring they require, added, "it's also like another layer on your business, shipping, out of state taxes, keeping inventory on the site synced with your store, etc... there's a lot to it, but when it works, it's worth it!"

"So, long story short, if you want to take up the challenge of an ecommerce site, then it can definitely help you increase sales IF you put the right advertising behind it. And if you don't want to do that right now, then the website should at least help you bring in new visitors..."

"IF I put the right advertising behind it," Eva finished Ethan's sentence.

"Exactly!"

Before wrapping up, Eva pressed for a ballpark price for the site, with and without ecommerce. Surprisingly, they gave her two prices without the hemming and hawing that she expected from a sales meeting. Without ecommerce the site would be $4500. With, it was going to be $6500. She had a lot to think about that night. This was a big decision, but she knew that the longer she put off the site the more customers she was missing.

CHAPTER 5: THE RISK OF DOING IT ON YOUR OWN

Risk: High
Reward: Short-term cost savings
Customer Journey: Applies to all stages

Before she left the downtown parking garage Eva texted Jessica to meet up for dinner at the new pop up food truck park a few blocks over, a new initiative from the downtown association to attract more foot traffic to the downtown area. Jessica Langmire was more than Eva's best office friend. They had weathered Jessica's divorce, Eva's mom passing, and a few failed romances together, and they were long overdue for some bad food and had a lot of catching up to do. When they spotted each other at the parking lot turned food court, Jessica goaded Eva about leaving her to fend for herself in the corporate quicksand of her soon to be former workplace. "Well, as my apology for stranding you in the healthcare hellscape, I'll buy you something you'll probably regret later."

"Ahh... heartburn goes great with heart ache," Jessica replied, laughing.

They surveyed the choices in front of them. Bravo Biscuits was dedicated to all things biscuity that could be produced in a 5x15 trailer. Biscuits and gravy, chicken biscuits, and a meatball biscuit were among the top sellers. Roll With It had a selection of fresh made sushi rolls and Hot Tamale had, you guessed it: Tamales. Not to limit their audience though, Hot Tamales also offered medium and mild tamales. After looking over all the options Eva and Jessica agreed that Nacho Nachos (pronounced "not yo nachos") was the best option. They offered a build your nachos item, customizable from the chips to the toppings.

As Eva looked around the parking lot she began to wonder if there were other reasons besides the menu that led them to Nacho Nachos. They both loved sushi after all. However, the Roll with It truck looked a little run down. It didn't look like the operator put a lot of effort into it and the name that was painted on the side of the truck had obviously been a weekend project for the owner. While she appreciated the hustle, she wasn't sure if she trusted sushi from the DIY project. Nacho Nachos on the other hand, had a vibrant wrap that caught their attention and also proudly advertised that they had a 4.9 star rating on Google, and their menu was well thought out and creatively displayed. There was just something about it that said, "Choose me!" So they had.

As they sat down with their Nacho Nachos, Jessica claimed a small portion of Eva's BBQ chicken nacho masterpiece that she had built as part of her career change redemption. The obvious news of the day was Marley's. Eva told Jessica the whole story from the beginning. About the time that she had caught Jessica up to her current marketing dilemma, Jessica had nearly finished her Nacho Nachos. "So, my next big decision is what to do about this website situation. It's kind of scary, because that's a big chunk of money to spend on something I am unsure of." Jessica nodded in agreement as Eva continued, "but on the other hand, if it DOES work, then it wouldn't take long for it to pay itself off."

Eva had a lot to tell and had barely touched her food, so as Jessica contemplated what sort of advice she could give her friend, Eva dug into her nachos, being careful to save a portion for Jessica as a peace offering. "Whenever I shop online, the better and more user-friendly the site is, the better chance I will buy something and be a return shopper. Oh, and I love it when they send coupons for things that are totally my style!" referring to the automated emails sent through the ecommerce systems of those sites. "So," she continued "I can see how having a good website could help you make some money." Jessica paused long enough to grab her portion of the BBQ chicken nachos, and continued with a half-full mouth and a little more animation. "I have the perfect analogy! Do you remember that old car I got in the divorce?"

"Oh yeah!" Eva exclaimed "That thing was a piece o' junk!"

Jessica replied, "Exactly! But it got me to where I needed to go... Until it didn't and it left me stranded in Kansas when I tried to drive it to visit my grandma." Eva nodded along with a doubtful expression on her face. Jessica, defensively replied "Trust me. You'll see where this is going. Your dad's website is that old car. And up till now (at best), it has got him where he needed to go, but now you are about to take it on a new adventure and you don't want it leaving you stranded in the middle of nowhere, with no cell service on I-70 thumbing for a ride."

By this time, Eva was nearly choking on her food as she was laughing, remembering the whole story of the ill-fated voyage of Jessica's old jalopy. "But wait, there's more!" Jessica interjected between snorts of laughter from Eva. "Every time anyone gets to buy a car they have two risks. If they buy a newer, more reliable car, the risk is up front. It's going to cost more and that's the obvious risk. Some people choose to go the other route and get an older, cheaper car. And this could be a good choice for them, IF they know how to fix it and have the time to do it. Otherwise they wind up losing money in the long run."

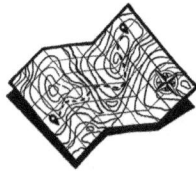

Determining what you can do on your own and what you need professional help with in your marketing can increase the efficiency of your marketing efforts. If you have the right skills, knowledge, and time for a particular task then it makes sense to tackle that on your own. However, some things might fall beyond the point of diminishing return for your marketing efforts. The good news about our era is that you can learn to do anything in digital marketing as long as you are good Googler and have a lot of time.

There are also several resources that are free or low cost that can help you up your digital marketing game - from low-cost monthly subscriptions to the full Adobe Suite (something that would have cost thousands of dollars a decade ago), to Canva, to a host of website builder platforms. If you decide to do things on your own, YouTube can also be your best friend, because there is a good chance that if you are having trouble figuring something out, someone else has already figured it out and made a video showing you how to do it. If a marketer, web designer, or social media expert is honest with you, they will tell you that even they Google a lot, because no one can know it all. The internet has helped a global population pool its knowledge on these subjects and offer solutions free of charge, but a certain level of skill is still required to sift through the results to find the best answers.

It's good to remember that any amount of DIYing you do for your business whether its marketing, accounting, or even the plumbing, should be a temporary skill that will become obsolete for you as your business grows. Marketing collateral and tactics that will persist for longer periods (your website, YouTube videos, branding, etc) will have a larger impact on your long term marketing than something that is more ephemeral, like a single social media post, and may require that you are involved in its production and maintenance beyond your initial investment in it.

When I was younger, I purchased a lemon car. Every other month, something new broke, leaked, or busted on it. We didn't have a lot of money to keep fixing it so I decided to trade it in for something that I could maintain on my own. After some shopping around, I became the proud owner of a blue 1964 Super Beetle. It was tiny, loud, and smelled like gasoline, but at that time, I figured that I could get a Haynes manual, invest in a new set of wrenches, and do whatever needed to be done to my own little Herbie. I remember the simplicity of the engine - no computers or sensors. Initially I had some small victories - changing the transmission fluid, changing the spark plugs. Me and Herbie had a good ole time, until, one fateful winter night as I was attempting to jump the car off. I had it parked half in the garage with our Subaru behind it and jumper cables strung through the snow into the backseat under which Herbie's battery was struggling to survive the cold winter. Earlier that day I had replaced the fuel filter. I did everything that the manual recommended or so I had thought. Why Herbie caught fire that night is still a mystery, but I suspect it had something to do with me spilling gasoline while changing the filter. I had my head down below the steering wheel trying to find something to add some pressure to the gas pedal so that the engine would idle (I still hadn't figured that one out) when my friend Greg yelled "Fire!" I looked up and saw flames shooting out of the rear of the car where the engine was. The car was still half in the garage with another car behind it so I yelled as loud as I could for my family to get out as I threw the Subaru in reverse and quickly backed it up, dragging the jumper cables with me.

Greg and I rolled Herbie out from under the garage and by that time my neighbor Doug came out to see the commotion. The three of us proceeded to scoop snow from the area surrounding the car and toss it onto the fire. Luckily we were able to put out the flames before the fire truck arrived.

The moral of this story.... DIYing might cost you more in the long run. However, if you consider yourself somewhat tech-savvy and have some extra time on your hands, then this could be a good option for you. If you have trouble with email or figuring out how to set up a social media profile, then you might save yourself a lot of time and frustration to hire someone for this. If you decide to attempt any elements of your marketing on your own, then I'd advise you to seek a very honest and objective opinion about your design.

The Roll With It food truck operator probably got some encouraging feedback and a false sense of confidence from his friends and family that led at least one customer that we know of to steer clear of what might have been the best sushi they ever had. A good question to ask yourself when you do any marketing yourself is "does this look like I've done it myself?" If the answer is yes, then maybe rethink your approach lest the story you tell with your marketing doesn't match the quality of your product or service. Remember, *you will either do business because of your marketing or in spite of it.*

Another approach you might consider taking is having someone on your team help with some aspects of your marketing. If you have a large enough team where you can have one person dedicated to certain marketing tasks such as social media or design, then leaning on them to carry out those tasks is ideal. However, just because they are young or know their way around a computer doesn't mean they are good at design or marketing. Once in a blue moon you might have hired someone as a receptionist that can do those other tasks with enough proficiency to help your business grow, but it's ideal to look for someone with those skills and experience during the hiring process.

As Eva drove home that evening she realized that while it was possible for her to do some things on her own, it might not help and could even hurt her business goals. The previous evening she had got online and experimented with what seemed to be the best DIY website builders she could find. They each had a lot of bells and whistles but she realized that for her it would be like the sushi truck signage.

Although it was a big investment, she felt that having a well designed website would pay off so when she returned home she pulled up the email from Web Monkeys with the quote and contract and e-signed it. She had a new excitement about her marketing and was eager to reap the rewards.

CHAPTER 6: THE SOCIAL MEDIA MOUNTAIN

Priority: Medium
Customer Journey: Brand Awareness and Consideration

Eva pulled the lid down on the Keurig and heard the pop of the pod inside. The transition from her old job to running a business made for late nights and early mornings. There was a lot to get done and the caffeine boiling around in that little plastic cup was her lifeline to make it through hump day. She yawned as the machine spurted out the last of the coffee into her cup with a hefty display of growling and hissing. Her phone interrupted her moment of zen as she was taking in the predawn sky out of the kitchen window. She looked down at the screen and saw it was an email from Ethan at Web Monkeys. The preview on her screen read "Welcome aboard! When is a good time to meet?" Eva became invigorated with a sense of determination, knowing that those late nights and early mornings would start paying off soon!

She promptly replied to the email and suggested that afternoon at 4. Her office was throwing a going away party for her after lunch and she was going to take advantage of the relaxed atmosphere and head out early. As she drove to the Nova Health Alliance headquarters she heard a new noise on her phone. When she got to the parking garage she looked down to see a notification from Facebook. Someone had left a review on her page. Her excitement quickly turned into a sinking feeling in her stomach. 1 star? "How could someone say Marley's was 1 star?!" she thought to herself. She read the full review...

"We drove an hour this morning to get a last minute gift and the store was closed. Their hours on here say 8-5 M-F. Thanks for ruining my niece's birthday!"

The store had, in fact, been closed for several days at that point, while Eva was transitioning out of her old job and preparing to jump into the role of shopkeeper full time. Even still, she felt a mixture of guilt for not putting some sort of message on the website or social media and anger at the customer's ungraciousness. Eva wanted to respond with the thoughts that were brewing in her head. They would definitely set this customer in their place, but knew it would be better to approach this later when she had a cooler head. In the meantime she bumped social media up in priority on her to-do list. Perhaps she could pick Ethan's brain about it this afternoon, she thought to herself.

There wasn't much to do at her job with only two full days left. She filed some overdue paperwork, set up an appointment with HR to review her employment exit checklist the next day, and reviewed a few projects that she would be handing off when she left. Around one o'clock everyone in her office shuffled into the conference room, where a cake that read "We'll Miss You Eva!" awaited them on the long polished table. She was greeted with encouraging "I'm so excited for you"s and a "will you be offering an ex-coworker discount?" from Davis, the office comedian.

After a minute or two of awkward mingling, Richard, her department supervisor, called everyone's attention and took a moment to laud Eva's accomplishments during her career at Nova and convey everyone's wishes for her success as she takes over her family business.

"Running your own business is not an easy task," he explained to the group. "My father ran a construction business in my hometown and he worked night and day to make sure jobs were finished on time and his crew got paid. And don't even get me started on hiring people. Hopefully, you will do better with that than we've done here," he said jokingly. "In all seriousness, our team is amazing, but it's going to be a little less so without you on it Eva."

At that the room clapped and there was a whistle or two before her friend Jessica piped up and told the room directly, "Hey you all, talk is cheap, but the good news is so are your likes and shares on social media. Everyone in here better get on their phones and like the Marley's Facebook page and follow them on Instagram before you leave! I will be checking your devices at the door!"

At that, Eva jumped in and said, "We don't actually have an Instagram yet, but please like our Facebook page. And, if you've ever bought anything from us in the past we could sure use some 5 star reviews!"

"Ever the marketer," Richard added, "Now get some cake and get back to work!"

"How are you not on Instagram yet?" Jessica questioned Eva after she had said her goodbyes to the coworkers that were more acquaintances than friends. "I was trying to set you up for a major following boost from all these hipsters." They both chuckled at the thought of their office mates as hipsters.

"I know. I have to get my social media act together. I just got a one star review on Facebook because our hours were wrong!" Eva confided with more exasperation than she wanted to show at an office party.

"Well, my dad, the fount of wisdom that he is, always used to say 'the solution to pollution is dilution,'" Jessica comforted her as she whipped out her phone and began typing. A few seconds later Eva's phone made that new sound again. Hesitantly she looked at the review notification: You received a 5 star review "best damn toy store in Georgia!" From Jessica.

Eva laughed, " Your dad is a very wise man indeed. Did he work for the EPA or something?"

"No," Jessica answered. "He was a pastor and had to dilute many a church committee," she said as finished off her piece of cake.

Eva looked at her watch. It was 3:15. She needed to make her exit if she was going to make it to the website meeting on time. Luckily there were only a few people picking at the vegetable tray and cake still. She gave them hugs on her way out and headed back to Burlington.

The website meeting was fairly quick. She had sent Ethan some sites that inspired her. They discussed what sections and pages she would need and Ethan asked questions that gave him a general direction to go in. "Alright, I think we've got enough info to get this ball rolling. I should have the initial design for your review within 2 weeks. If you like it then I'll send it on to be developed which should take 2-3 more weeks," Ethan told her as they were heading out.

"Before I go, can I pick your brain about something?" Eva asked.

"Of course! What do you need to know?" Ethan replied.

"Social media... how do I do it?" she asked, somewhat embarrassed by her lack of knowledge. They both laughed at her candor.

"Well, that's a big question and probably one we can't answer quickly." Ethan continued, "Usually businesses have a few options. They can hire an agency to manage it all for them. Typically this only pays off for larger brands that can afford to do it well. I've seen smaller businesses pay a lot for social media management and they never see a return off of it. However, if they have someone on staff that can run it and understands people, how people react online, and can take a decent photo with their phone then that's the sweet spot. Your own people will always beat an agency when you're a local business."

Eva jumped in and cut to the chase, knowing that it was close to closing time, "What if I don't have either of those options, I'm not exactly sure how Instagram works, or if I need a Twitter or not?"

Ethan responded, "It sounds like what you might need is a simple social media consultation. We have someone we work with that can sit down with you, show the ropes, and give you what you need to do it on your own or at least make good social media decisions. Want me to connect you two?"

"That sounds like it's exactly what I need!" Eva replied enthusiastically.

As Eva was walking back to the shop, she felt her phone buzz. She pulled it from her pocket and saw an email notification. She opened the email while she was waiting for the crosswalk sign to change. The message was from a Lainey S.:

"Hi Eva,
Ethan from Web Monkeys told me you might be interested in a social media consultation. I work with a lot of local businesses in and around the Atlanta area and would love to help you out too. The link to book an appointment is below. I charge $150/hour and most of the time our consultations only take 1 or 2 hours at most. During our first consultation, I would love to hear about your business and what some of your goals are, then I can help you build a plan to get there with your social media. Let me know if you have any questions!
~Lainey"

She looked up and realized she had missed the signal and the crosswalk sign was counting down, so she jogged across the street. She wanted to make it to the shop before it got too late. Tomorrow was going to be the first day of this new chapter of her life and she wanted to take an inventory of what needed to be done. The shop had been closed for the last two weeks. She felt a sense of determination and exhilaration as she approached the shop. She pulled the worn out key that her father had given her out of her pocket and unlocked the door. The little bell at the top of the door jingled as she pushed it open. She stepped in and inhaled deeply, savoring the aroma of the aged wood of the old building and the subtle scent of time-worn books.

As she looked out over the shop she saw the familiar rows of shelves, each brimming with stories waiting to be discovered. The toys, ranging from handcrafted wooden figures to intricate mechanical puzzles and even the newest electronic novelties, were artfully displayed, casting playful shadows in the dim light. It was a scene straight out of a dream, a magical blend of nostalgia and imagination. In this moment, the shop felt like a sanctuary, a place untouched by the whirlwind she had been in since her father's heart attack, holding steadfast in its charm. She felt a connection to each item, a legacy left by her father, now hers to continue.

Eva moved through the quiet aisles of the shop, her footsteps echoing softly against the wooden floors. The dust that had settled during the shop's closure caught the light, creating a hazy, almost ethereal atmosphere. She ran her fingers over the spines of books. It was a collection curated with love and care, a reflection of a lifetime dedicated to bringing joy and knowledge to others. The shop, though filled with charm, bore the silent marks of time and inattention, the natural outcome of her father's slowing pace over the years.

Surveying the space, Eva realized the potential it held, a potential that was yet to be fully tapped. The digital age had transformed the landscape of commerce and communication, and she knew that to revive and sustain Marley's, she needed to embrace these changes. The need for a social media strategy was clear to her now. She imagined that their social media would not only showcase the unique offerings of the shop but also weave together its rich history and the joyful stories of its customers.

Social media, she pondered, could be the bridge between the shop's timeless charm and the dynamic, fast-paced world outside its doors. It could connect her with a community that valued not just the products, but the stories they held. This, she thought, could be the key to ushering the shop into a new era, but there was so much she didn't know about how it all works.

She quickly pulled out her phone to book an appointment with Lainey. She had already determined that $150-300 was a small price to pay to help her understand how to use this tool to grow her business. When she opened the booking link she noticed that there was an appointment slot for 5pm that evening, 10 minutes away. "No time like the present!" she thought to herself as she booked the appointment. She also was grateful for the weird business hours of freelancers. Luckily, she had her laptop with her, and 10 minutes later she was logging into the video conferencing link that Lainey had sent.

When Lainey opened the meeting, she saw Eva inside a dimly lit toy shop and it immediately sparked her interest. "Well, that was fast!" Lainey said, laughing over the swiftness with which Eva had booked the appointment.

Eva laughed, saying, "Tell me about it! My whole life has been fast the last few weeks. Two weeks ago, I was advancing my career in a corporate medical office, now I am the new owner of a book and toy shop! So, I am a little in over my head with the marketing side of things and Ethan said you are a social media extraordinaire. Help!" Eva's vulnerability and honesty lightened the mood a little.

Lainey responded, "Well, that's exactly what I hope to do. Ethan told me a little about your situation and I had a brief moment to look over your website and social media." Eva's face cringed slightly at the thought of her current site and social profiles being judged by a professional. "Don't worry," Lainey assured her, "They aren't great, but I've definitely seen worse. The good news is that your business has a lot of potential to get a lot of reach on social media."

Eva interrupted her, "I've heard that term before, reach. What do you mean by that exactly?"

Lainey looked excited to answer. "Reach is the number of unique people who are seeing your content on social. The higher that number the better. Typically, engaging content gets more reach, and since your business piques the curiosity of young and old alike, I think you can do very well with it."

They continued on and Lainey described the types of photos that would work well on Facebook and Instagram and convinced her that Tik Tok could be a very profitable channel for her to explore. They also discussed whether she should outsource her social media or not. Since Eva's marketing budget was very limited this first year, Lainey recommended that she put in the work to do it on her own and then next year reexamine it to see if it's worth hiring an agency or person to do it for her. After two hours, she had the basics of her social media strategy down:

- Clean up existing accounts: Get the new logo as the profile pic, make sure hours and information are correct, and change out any old/bad header photos.

- Create an Instagram account

- Invite all her personal connections to follow and like her accounts

- Create a TikTok account

- Post to Facebook and Instagram at least 3 times a week.

- Use photos with people in them as much as possible.

- Hire someone who is familiar with Tik Tok and can help create engaging content every week as part of their job.

Eva closed her laptop after saying goodbye to Lainey. It was getting dark outside, but the adrenaline of the moment was still rushing through Eva's blood so she decided to stay at the shop and prepare it for her inaugural day. She made a list of all the things that needed to be cleaned, fixed, or added to the store. Later that evening, she could hear music from the bar down the street as she locked up. The cool night air was at her back as she walked towards the parking garage. With a renewed sense of purpose and an optimistic smile, she began to envision the bright future for this enchanted place.

Like some of the other risks so far, the biggest danger with social media is wasting time and/or money, things that most local businesses don't have a lot of to spare. However, the risk you run when you're not active on social media is a lack of relevance, brand awareness, and reach with your target audience. More than any other tool in your marketing kit, social media changes almost daily. New platforms emerge, new tools within existing platforms are launched or change, and the rules surrounding all of them are in constant flux. It's an easy wilderness to get lost in. In fact, between the time this book is published and you are reading it, there will be any number of changes and probably a new platform launched. So, rather than getting into specifics, we will stick with some broader rules that should apply for a year or so at least (no guarantees).

As I am writing this book, the social media world looks as follows:

- Facebook continues to be a juggernaut in the social media world, boasting over 2.9 billion monthly active users as of early 2023. Its widespread use across various age groups makes it a versatile platform for businesses aiming to reach a broad audience. Instagram, with its visually driven content, has also seen significant growth, especially among younger demographics, with over 1.4 billion monthly active users. This platform is particularly effective for businesses that can leverage visual storytelling, such as those in food, fashion, and tourism.

- LinkedIn remains the premier platform for professional networking, with over 810 million users, and is a valuable resource for B2B marketing and professional brand building.

- X, formally known as Twitter, with its real-time information and conversation-driven format, has a user base of about 396 million, and is the hub for politics, reporting, financial news, and celebrities. Few local businesses will benefit much from a presence on X.

- TikTok has emerged as the dark horse of the social media world in the last few years and disrupted the social media landscape with short-form video content, attracting over 1 billion users, predominantly from Gen Z and younger millennials. This platform's creative and trend-driven nature provides unique opportunities for businesses to tap into viral marketing and reach younger consumers. While Facebook, Instagram, and even YouTube have tried to catch up to TikTok with short form video, they are still far behind in user engagement and the amount of time spent on the platform.

- Lastly, platforms such as Snapchat and Pinterest, with 557 million and 433 million monthly active users respectively, continue to hold their niche in the market. Snapchat is popular among younger audiences for its ephemeral content, while Pinterest is a haven for inspiration seekers, particularly popular in categories like home decor, DIY, and fashion.

You need to be on some of the platforms no matter what. Having a Facebook page is the equivalent of putting on your pants before going out of the house. If you have a business, you better have a Facebook page, even if it sucks. Likewise, if you are a B2B business, LinkedIn is a must have. Even if they exist simply so other people can tag you in their own posts, you need them.

To help you determine which platforms make the most sense for your business to invest more time or resources on, consider these things:

- Where are most of your customers spending most of their time online?

- Which platform do you think you can create great content for consistently?

- Are there any opportunities to break into a new market through one of these platforms?

Social media is going to help you with the first two stages of your customer journey. It can be one of the first times someone encounters your brand (awareness), or it can be a touchpoint before they make a purchase (whether they are a new or returning customer). With most awareness tactics, the main metric that you can go by is reach. Reach is the number of unique individuals who have seen your content. The more reach you have, the more people are becoming aware of your brand. The good news is that engaging content tends to get more reach because people are liking, commenting, and sharing it. However, if your content is getting a lot of engagement but not a lot of reach, you need to examine why.

One potential reason could be that your content is narrowly focused on a small audience who is highly engaged with the sort of content you have. It can be good to see all the likes and comments, but ultimately you want more people to see your content, so reach is the number you want to keep track of. It will help you gauge whether your social media content is working or not.

To find more resources for social media and influencer marketing, including step by step guides, and the up to date information, scan this QR code or visit theclimb.guide/social

Here are a couple of principles that will help your content be engaging and increase reach:

- Use photos with people in them. Currently, most of the algorithms will give a small preference to photos with faces. You can get photos of customers, people at networking events, etc.

- Tag people or other businesses in your posts as much as you appropriately can. When people are tagged, they will usually respond with some amount of engagement and it also allows your content to appear in the feeds of their network.

- Use photos of pets. If you have a good reason to get a dog, cat, or other animal in your posts, do it. The old adage, "fur sells", is true. It also gets a log of engagement on social media.

- Learn the basics of composition and lighting. With the camera abilities of phones today, there is no reason why you cannot have amazing photos on your social media. Get familiar with the settings on your phone that will help you take great photos and videos.

Influencer Marketing:

If you operate a business to consumer (B2C) business, then you might consider influencers as an effective brand awareness tactic. Influencers typically have a sizable following in a particular niche, with whom they actively engage. When influencer marketing first became popular, many brands would often trade with the influencer in exchange for posts about their products or services. However, as influencers have realized the value of their work, most require monetary compensation along with trades. Since influencer marketing is a brand awareness tactic, it's easiest to understand their value in terms of the amount of reach and impressions they can generate for your brand. Since not all influencers are the same, and some have much more influence over their followers than others, there isn't a flat price that can accurately be applied to the value they bring. However, I recommend starting with $20-30 per thousand (CPM) impressions. That means anytime one thousand people see their posts about your brand, it's worth about $20-30 to you. If you can get your impressions for less than that, you're getting a good deal. If the influencer wants to charge more than $30 CPM, it might be worth it, but you'd need to make sure before investing too much.

Pitfall Warning:

Don't chase too hard after trends. If you were to create a TikTok video for every trend that came around, that's all you would do. And chances are, it wouldn't help you get to your goal. There is a romanticism about 'going viral' and having that video of your office doing the chicken dance get 100K+ reactions. You might even see some of your competition participating in trends that get them a lot of engagement, but unless it's relatively easy to do, or you have a clear strategic goal for it in mind, then most of the time,chasing trends will just be busy work with little reward. Focus more on content that is engaging independent of trends and raises the profile of your brand.

CHAPTER 7: YOUR COMMUNITY RESUME

Priority: Medium
Customer Journey: Awareness and Consideration

At this point Eva was about 2 weeks into her new role as full time shop owner at Marley's Home for Wayward Books and Gifted Toys. Her new social media plan was beginning to gain some traction. Old customers who had liked the Facebook page years ago started to take notice and share the news of the new name and ownership. They loved the candid photos of Eva and her dad demoing the new toys as they'd get them in. She even had a few new faces come to the store for specific toys they had seen on Facebook and Instagram. One such customer was Brian, a middle-aged father of two. He had come in because he saw a post on Facebook that said they had started to carry the raspberry-pi computer kits for kids, and he thought it would be a great way to get his two pre-teens to learn a new skill.

Brian was relatively new to town. It took most outsiders a few years before Burlingtonians considered them fully integrated. He moved to Burlington because he was hired as the new membership director at Burlington's Chamber of Commerce. As he was checking out, he introduced himself as such and asked

Eva if she had considered rejoining the chamber. "Rejoin?" she thought to herself. She knew how much her dad loved the community and so the fact that Marley's wasn't a chamber member any more came as a surprise to her. She did not let this come across her face, but rather said, "I am very interested. Do you have a card? I can get in touch when we are ready." He took a plain looking business card out and handed it to her and thanked her for the great gift for his kids as he left. She put the card in her pocket and made a mental note to ask her dad why they weren't still members.

She had just enough time before a scheduled interview with Chris Brown, a potential new clerk, to check her email as she scanned the modest kitchen area in the back for something to eat. Surrendering to the fast paced entrepreneurial lifestyle, she threw some instant oatmeal in the microwave. She scanned the 20 new emails in her inbox with a finely tuned ability to ignore the spammy "Reach your best customers with our new social media, click funnel, engine!" ones. And then she saw one that made her perk up. It was from Ethan. The subject: Website Design is Ready for Review! She opened it anxiously and quickly read Ethan's message:

"Hi Eva, The link below will take you to the prototype of your site. Keep in mind that those words and some of the images are placeholders, so don't get startled if you see Latin on the 'about us' page. We still need to get that content from you ;-) Here is the link to send us the content for some of the pages as well as the link to the prototype. When is a good time to meet with us to review?"

Eva had totally forgotten that she was supposed to get Web Monkeys some of the info and images for the site. But she didn't let that ruin the excitement of the moment. She clicked on the prototype link and was thrilled to see that Ethan had nailed it! Everything about the site was Marley's through and through. She started to understand how her brand could be something that went beyond her logo and infused everything about her business. After she clicked through all the pages and explored the new online home of her shop, she hit 'Forward' on the email and added Staci to the recipient field with the message "OMG! Thank you for sending me to Web Monkeys! The new site design is beautiful!"

She hit the reply button on the original email and told Ethan "The site looks amazing! Go ahead and proceed, no need to review."

As she settled in behind the counter, she heard the signature jingle of the shop's door bell as Chris entered the store with a look of timidity and an air of optimism. "You must be Chris," she said, as he awkwardly waved hello.

"Yes, I am here for an interview."

Eva sat across from Chris in the small office at the back of the shop. The room was filled with the nostalgic charm of the shop, shelves lined with toys from different eras. She had been looking for someone to bring a fresh perspective to the shop, and Chris's application stood out. His resume noted that he helped a few other businesses with their digital marketing to help pay his way through school, a skill set and work ethic that Eva knew could be invaluable for the shop.

As the interview commenced, Eva was immediately struck by Chris's enthusiasm and his unique blend of traditional and modern viewpoints. "Chris, tell me, what makes you want to join the Marley's team? What do you think you can bring to the table?" she asked.

Chris, dressed smartly but with a playful edge, replied, "Honestly, I used to come here as a kid all the time and this place holds a lot of memories for me, but I have seen it wind down over the years and now I can see you bringing this place back to life. I want to help with that and I think I can bring some of my digital marketing skills to help."

Eva nodded, impressed. She probed further, "Can you give me an example of how you would apply your digital marketing skills here?"

Chris leaned forward, his eyes lighting up with ideas. "Absolutely. For starters, we could enhance the shop's online presence, starting with social media platforms. Right now Marley's isn't on TikTok and I think it could get a lot of local followers easily. I am also really good at figuring tech things out. Give me a technical or marketing problem and with a little time on Google, I can figure it out."

Eva listened intently, already picturing the positive changes Chris could bring. "I love your confidence and the skills that you could bring to our team. We are definitely trying to figure out all the social media platforms. But what about the in-store experience? How would you ensure it complements our digital efforts?"

Chris's response was thoughtful. "The in-store experience is where the magic happens. It's about creating an environment where kids and parents feel the wonder of discovering new toys. I envision interactive displays, maybe even small events in the shop that can be promoted online. It's all about creating a seamless experience that merges the digital with the physical."

As the interview concluded, Eva felt a sense of certainty. Chris not only had the skills but also the passion and vision that aligned perfectly with the ethos of Marley's.

Chris left with a cheery farewell, right before the phone rang. She picked it up, "Hello, thanks for calling Marley's Home for Wayward Books and Gifted Toys! How can I help you?"

The caller replied, "Hi, may I speak to the owner?"

"This is her." Eva replied.

"Hi, I am calling on behalf of the Burlington Elementary Tee-Ball League to see if you would like to renew your sponsorship for this upcoming season."

The Importance of Your Second Resume

When I was growing up, my dad was a Methodist pastor. This meant that every 3-5 years we shuffled around East Tennessee to a new church. Most of these appointments were in small towns and I was able to experience many different communities. They each have their own personalities, but one common thread that runs through all of them is pride in their community and a strong desire to help their neighbors. That's why being present in the community and supporting important programs is vital to thriving as a small business.

At some point you will be approached to sponsor an event, a club, a kid, something. And you will need to make a business decision. Do you have money to simply give away? If yes, then great!, but if not you'll have to make a decision that will affect your budget. Will that sponsorship help get your brand in front of the right people better? How long will it be seen and by how many people? Are the sponsorship benefits clearly listed? It might seem harsh to analyze it like this, but a paid sponsorship is a business advertising decision and should be determined with your marketing plan. If none of that sits right with you, then simply consider it a donation and don't expect anything from it. The more you can associate your name with good causes in your community, the stronger your brand will be. Consider these opportunities:

- Is there a non-profit organization in your town that is related to your industry in some form or fashion?

- Are there partnerships with local schools and/or sports teams that align with your brand?

- Serving on a non-profit board or on a committee can help build your rapport in the community and connect you with influential people that can be advocates for your business.

In our community here in East Tennessee, we often say you have a professional resume and a community resume. What does your community resume say about your business? Is it a pillar in the community? If not, then consider the steps you can take to make it so. You not only improve the profile of your brand, you also help make your community a better place to live.

Chambers of commerce are also great ways to get connected into your local community. Whether you are a B2C or B2B business, it doesn't matter. The people who tend to frequent networking events also tend to know a lot of people. Malcolm Gladwell calls this crowd Connectors because they know people who know people. They are the ones who tell their friends about a restaurant and those friends tell their friends. They might not need your product or service, but they know someone who does.

Chambers are like the towns they are in. Each one has its own personality, its own strengths and its own weaknesses. Epic Nine has had the opportunity to be a member of 8 different chambers, and each one helped us in its own way. My favorite chambers are the ones that offer small businesses regular (monthly or bi-monthly) ways to connect and network. These opportunities typically come in the form of a morning coffee or an afternoon 'Business After Hours'. When clients come in for an initial consultation with us, many times we tell them to join the chamber before they spend any other marketing dollars. However, your chamber membership is only as good as the extent that you use it. Taking advantage of the opportunities your local chamber gives you are important. Here are a few ways to do that:

- Attend as many networking events as possible. This includes coffees, business after hours, ribbon cuttings, and other special events.

- Take photos with other business people at these events and tag them on social media.

- Always have business cards with you.

- Try to collect as many business cards as you can at networking events and develop a system to keep track of the people you follow up with.

Remember when you're at a networking event, that a lot of the people there feel awkward and aren't 'good at networking'. Be the one to start a conversation. Ask someone questions about themselves. It's a great way to build rapport.

If you are interested in more ways your business can help nonprofits in your community scan the QR Code or visit theclimb.guide/community

Networking Groups:

Networking groups like Business Networking International (BNI) and Networking Today have become a vital tool for many professionals. The structured environment of BNI is particularly beneficial for those who are new to networking or prefer a more formal approach to building business connections. Members have the opportunity to expand their network across various industries, leading to a rich diversity of contacts. Notably, BNI is known for its focus on generating referral business, which is a significant advantage for members. Picture a bustling room filled with individuals from legal, financial, home services, and marketing businesses, each bringing a unique set of skills and experiences to the table. This is the essence of BNI - a melting pot of opportunities and connections.

However, there are certain considerations to bear in mind. Membership in groups like BNI involves fees, which can be a deciding factor for small businesses or individual entrepreneurs. The commitment is not just financial but also temporal, with regular meetings and the expectation to actively contribute to the referral system. One unique aspect of BNI is its policy of allowing only one representative per professional specialty in each chapter. While this reduces direct competition, it can also limit opportunities for those in more common industries. Furthermore, there is an inherent pressure to provide referrals, which might sometimes lead to recommending businesses out of obligation rather than confidence.

Networking groups like these could be very profitable for you, if the group chemistry is right. However, you should take advantage of free visits to evaluate the chemistry of the group. If you see a lot of referrals being passed, an energetic spirit with members, and the meeting is not boring or awkward, then it might be a good source of referrals. If the group chemistry isn't there though, don't waste your time or money.

On her way home that evening, Eva called her dad. "Dad, why didn't you renew your chamber membership?"

"Oh, that," he said, "Well, I guess I just didn't see the need for it over the last few years. They came around for renewals a few years back when things were tight and I just put it off. I guess I just forgot to pick it back up again."

Once she got home and threw the leftovers from the night before in the oven, she considered how she could use the chamber membership and tee-ball sponsorship to grow the business. She knew that the chamber was very active in the local economy and a lot of the members worked hard to support other local businesses. She remembered seeing some of her friends from high school posting pictures at some of the other local businesses on Small Business Saturday last year. The membership fee was relatively small ($350 a year) compared to some of her other marketing expenses, so she decided to call Brian in the morning and see what the perks of membership were.

She knew she was going to renew the tee ball sponsorship, but she wondered if there was a way to do more than simply have the logo on the back of a shirt. She began thinking about her goals and her target audience. Her dad definitely knew his target audience was the kids on these baseball teams. But things had changed and it was a little harder to excite kids with the toys in their shop as it had been. What was something that could get these kids in the door? She called up the family expert on all things pre-teen, her brother Michael. After the usual small talk, she asked him "What do kids get excited about these days that doesn't involve a phone or tablet?"

Without hesitating, Michael responded, "Roblox".

"Roblox? What is that, like legos?"

He laughed, "Not exactly. It's a computer game, but they also sell cards in the stores that are like little Roblox lottery tickets. When they open them up, they get a code that allows them access to items in the game that they couldn't otherwise get. Your niece loves them."

Eva thought back to the last time she was in the checkout line at Target. She remembered seeing these little baseball card-like packs with the Roblox logo on them. It wasn't extensive market research, but on her budget it would have to do. Besides, testing it out on a small sample like the local tee-ball league wouldn't hurt. When she got off the phone she emailed the tee-ball coordinator and asked, "If I sponsor the league, can we also make sure they get a discount at the store? I'd like to give each kid a free Roblox card with every purchase of $25 or more. All they have to do is wear their jersey to the store."

CHAPTER 8: LOCATION AND SIGNAGE

Risk: High (Location) Medium (Signage)
Reward: A great location can provide long term brand awareness and customer retention. Great signage helps in the Awareness and Consideration stages.
Customer Journey: Awareness and Consideration

The next morning Eva called Brian. "Hi Brian. This is Eva from Marley's."

"Oh, hey Eva, great to hear from you."

"I have some questions about membership. Marley's has always valued being supportive of the community and I believe being a member of the chamber is part of that. So, we're in. But I am curious, what are the perks of membership?"

Trying not to sound too excited about a fresh sale, Brian replied "That's great! You will not regret it. With the basic level of membership you get to come to all of our networking events, you get 2 sponsored social media posts from our account each year, and you can list any events or specials in our weekly member newsletter that goes out to our 1,500 members."

"Do you have anything that can help us get a little boost in our transition? My dad recently passed ownership to me and we changed the name. Do you offer any sort of PR services?"

"That sounds like you are in the perfect situation for a grand re-opening. We would publicize this as a chamber event, invite all the members to it, and then have a ribbon-cutting and celebration at your location."

"That sounds fantastic, how soon can we do that?"

Brian scrolled through his upcoming event calendar and said, "It looks like we have an opening in 3 weeks. Want to book it?"

"Yes!" Eva replied, "That sounds perfect. What else do you have?"

Brian paused to review all the available benefits and services of chamber membership in his head, "Oh, you can also host one of our networking events. You simply open your shop up one morning, supply coffee and snacks, and all the chamber members descend upon your location for networking and caffeine. It's a great way to keep your business in front of people."

"Sign me up!" Eva replied.

"Well, there is an additional $300 fee for that, and it doesn't look like we have an opening until December."

Eva knew that getting 50-100 people in her building would be help win them over as customers and help her reach goal #2 so she told Brian, "I'm in. Send me a bill and put us on the calendar for December!"

As she pulled up to the shop, she examined it like you do your house before having people over for a party. The storefront needed some help. A fresh coat of paint would help. The sign was dated and still had the old logo on it. She needed a new one with her new logo before the grand re-opening. She checked her recent calls and clicked on Brian's number again, "Hey Brian, it's me, Eva, again. Who do you recommend for signage?"

Everything about your business is telling a story. From the way you answer the phone, to how clean (or messy) your store is, even how manicured your parking lot area is. It is communicating little signals to your customers or would-be customers. It's either telling them a story that is drawing them in or one that is pushing them away. A lot of this happens on a subconscious level with your customers, but most of it is within your power to control. You get to craft the story your business is telling!

Signage is a big part of that story. When you pull up to the gas station that has a half-lit sign, or the restaurant that has a letter missing from the signage above the door, does this make you feel more or less confident about your decisions to go there? Just like there are touchpoints that can move people along the customer journey from 0 to 10, there are also touchpoints that can move people backwards along that journey. Bad signage is one of them. It won't move someone from a 10 to a 0, but it might move them from a 7 to a 5 and that's a big threat, especially considering the work you put in to move them from a 5 to a 7.

The classic example of this is a cafe that opened up in our downtown. The food and prices were amazing. It was one of my favorite places to have lunch. However, their sign looked like they had the local elementary school art class create it. After a few months of faithfully supporting them, I could see the writing on the wall. Most of the seats were empty every time I was in, and even after consistent goading, they never changed their sign. After another few months, they were out of business. I later heard from a colleague at a nearby college who would often host groups of leaders, that they had considered bringing some of those groups to that cafe for lunch, but never followed through because the signage made them second-guess it.

How your business appears, both inside and outside, can help you win or lose business. As you are able, make improvements to the customer experience in and around your business. Most often this can be tackled easily with physical changes, but also consider the signals your phone and email communication sends as well. How does your staff sound when they answer the phone? Do you have a well thought out voicemail message and system? Do your emails look professional with a professional signature, or do they come from a hotmail.com account?

The physical location of your business is also a risk you have to weigh carefully. If you have people coming to your location, this matters more than if you are more of an industrial business that does not have to appeal to the public. You've heard it before: "Location, Location, Location!". The emphasis is much warranted. The Great Smoky Mountains National Park happens to be close to our town. It is the most visited national park in the county with over 14 million people coming through it every year. Right next door to the national park is Sevier County, home to Dollywood,

Pigeon Forge, Gatlinburg and all the attractions and sights that have built up around them. In 2021 Sevier County's GPD was over $4 Billion. That's 'billion', with a 'B'. To put that in perspective, Sevier County's population is less than 100,000. Sevier County happens to be on one of the easiest entrances/exits of the national park. Location.

Now, if you are a business in Sevier County, being on that main thoroughfare can be the difference between huge profits or crushed dreams. Some of the businesses that are located on the main drag in Pigeon Forge don't have to be great to make money. They don't even have to be that good. One business that is located on the main road through Pigeon Forge has been there for over twenty years and has a 2.9 star rating on Google (out of 3500 reviews!). It continues to make money for one sole reason, location. Conversely, we have seen businesses have to shutter, because the location they chose was just too inconvenient to gain the traffic it needed to survive. When you consider all the expenses of your business, your lease might be one of the biggest single expenses outside of payroll. If you skimp on your location and go with something that is cheaper but not ideal, then you will probably make up the difference and then some with the amount of advertising you will need to drive business there.

While signage and location aren't typically considered part of your marketing budget, it's important to understand that they do impact the story you are telling to your customers and will have an effect on how well your other marketing works.

Amongst a storehouse of outdated cleaning supplies and random nuts and bolts, Eva found leftover paint for the outside trim in the basement of the shop. She popped the lid and stirred separated ingredients together until they formed a solid bright white. As the brush met the wooden frame of the door, it instantly breathed new life into the appearance of the shop. In a way it was emblematic of her marketing plan. She let her mind drift, imagining her shop as the hub of downtown, people entering the shop empty-handed, but leaving with their arms full of toys and books with smiles on their faces. Time was running out to make that a reality though. She knew that the world didn't sleep, no matter how small the town is where you find yourself. If she was going to meet her goals and make this shop work, she still had a lot to do. She leaned into the door and yelled for Chris, the new part time clerk to come outside. Chris was a second-year engineering student at the local college. He had grown up getting Marley's blocks and marble sets, and so working there was a dream come true. On slow days he would transform the demo marble roller coaster set into physics-defying works of art.

When he came outside, he found Eva on a ladder with paintbrush in hand. "Hurry, take a picture!" She playfully commanded him as she posed with a paint bucket and brush. "For Instagram," she added. "Can you post it and add the caption 'giving the shop front some much needed attention. Can't wait for the new sign to get here!"

Chris went back inside, smiling as he punched the caption into the Instagram post. As Eva continued painting, she felt her phone in her pocket buzzing periodically. Her hands were too messy with paint to check it and she nearly forgot about all the digital commotion until later that evening. When she pulled her phone out of her pocket she noticed she had more notifications from Instagram and Facebook than she could count. Between both platforms, the photo that Chris had posted for her had over 200 likes, a few shares, and comments from friends and strangers saying things like "Can't wait to bring my kids to this cool new store in downtown!" (she forgave the commenter for being oblivious to the shop for the previous 40 years - on the condition that she actually brings her kids!) and "Eva! The shop is so cute! I can't wait to visit you this summer!" Chris had not only posted it on the businesses accounts, but also tagged her in the picture. She wondered why none of her previous posts had garnered that much engagement. Looking back through them, she realized that this was one of the only images with a person in it, and definitely the only one with a person tagged in it. She made a mental note of that observation and resolved to post more people.

CHAPTER 9: THE RISKS OF ADVERTISING

Risk: High
Reward: If done correctly, the rewards from this risk will be consistent and high.
Customer Journey: Applies to all stages

"Advertisting troubles both sociologists and financial directors: the former because they think it works, the latter because they think it does not." - Bullmore

The next few weeks leading up to her grand re-opening, Eva's anticipation began to build. She was hoping for a story in the paper, and maybe even a news station. After all, the world could always use a feel good story about a father passing down the family business to his daughter. As a neighborly gesture, she had hired Beanology, the hipster coffee shop around the corner, to cater the event. The local sign company had just finished hanging the new sign the day before. It looked amazing, especially lit up at night. The day of the event came and Brian showed up early to get the registration table setup so that chamber staff could collect business cards for a raffle and give name tags for the attendees. Eva, her dad, and Chris were all there in traditional toy shop aprons. This was a new touch that Eva had implemented to bolster the ambiance of the shop.

Around 8:45, people started pouring in, dropping their business cards in the fish bowl, and congratulating Eva for the grand re-opening. Eva had given Chris specific instructions to get as many 'people photos' as he could so he could tag people in the shop's social media accounts. Chris had a ball getting selfies with chamber members, catching them in candid poses playing with the demo toys, and shaking hands with each other. As 9:15 drew close, Brain ushered everyone to the sidewalk outside where he had positioned the chamber officials with Eva and her dad and the ribbon. As the crowd quieted in anticipation, Eva's dad took the opportunity to tell them how proud he was of Eva. With tears in his eyes, he told them how she used to spend hours playing with the block sets in the store, building all sorts of castles and villages and now she is building something even greater with the business itself.

Eva jumped in and gave him the opportunity to brush a tear out of the corner of his eye and chuckle at his sentimentality, "Whatever success comes from Marley's, it's built on the foundation that my father has laid in this community. Thank you all for coming out here today to support us. We are excited about the next chapter of Marley's Home for Wayward Toys and Orphaned Books and hope we continue to spark the imagination of Burlington for at least a few more decades!"

The crowd applauded as Brian presented Eva with a pair of large golden scissors. He led the crowd in a countdown, "3, 2, 1." As the crowd shouted "one!" Eva cut the bright red ribbon in two.

Everyone clapped and took pictures before grabbing one more pastry from Beanology and heading to their day jobs. As they cleaned up, Brian mentioned that his kids loved the raspberry pi kits and when they get their birthday money next month they want to come spend it all in one place, Marley's! He handed her the stack of business cards from the fish bowl, "These are for you. If you do any email marketing, you can add them to it."

Eva felt overwhelmed by the support from the community as well as all the new opportunities ahead of her. She put a rubber band around the mostly uniform bundle of cards and threw them on her desk in the back. She knew that they were valuable, but she wasn't quite sure what to do with them yet. "Perhaps Chris could use them to tag businesses in social media posts," she thought to herself.

That evening, Eva's phone began to blow up with social media notifications. She could get used to that! Her strategy of adding a lot of people in her posts was paying off. Along with the Facebook and Instagram notices, she also received emails from chamber members who had attended and taken her card.

Two of them, Rodney Cantrell and Stephanie Wallace, were from local media companies: the local daily newspaper, The Burlington Herald, and a broadcast television station in the neighboring city, respectively. They wanted to have a meeting with her, to 'explore her options'. She knew that to be competitive she might have to purchase advertising from one or both of them, but she knew that there were "right things" and "right times". Blowing her whole advertising budget on a few ads might compromise her ability to reach her goals. However, she figured it couldn't hurt to hear them out.

She had already spent $7,500 of her dad's initial loan on the website and the new signage, so she had roughly $2,500 to spend on advertising (not counting the extra $400/month that they weren't paying WebCorp anymore) in the near future, but it had to prove itself. She knew that this was not something she could leave to chance. She was beginning to feel the uncertainty and the risk of marketing. None of it is guaranteed, she thought. It really is like aiming an arrow at a target as best you can and letting the string go. She emailed them both back and set up a time the next week for them to meet.

Just then the front bell rang and in walked a young boy and his mom. The boy was probably 8 with messy hair that had been plastered to his face through a day in the hot sun. He was wearing a Burlington Elementary Tee-Ball shirt. As he and his mom perused the aisles she saw the Marley's logo on the back. "Bullseye!" she thought to herself. That was the first, but definitely not the last sweaty tee-ball player she saw in the store that summer. All in all, over the course of the next few months, the small investment in a tee-ball sponsorship produced $1250 sales. Not a bad return.

Early the next week she had coffee with her friend Marie, who was also a local business owner. Marie operated Downtown Yoga, just a few blocks away from the shop. Dinners were getting harder to arrange since she had to be at the shop for the new longer hours. But she loved the newfound time for a good cup of coffee in the mornings. Being her own boss and not having to clock in at 8:00am, 45 minutes from home had its perks. Today that perk was a large house blend from Beanology and good conversation with Marie.

As to be expected, the hot topic was Eva's new venture. Marie was excited to talk shop and lend her entrepreneurial wisdom to Eva.

They sat down at a small table outside. Marie congratulated her on the ribbon cutting, "The grand reopening was on point. I went and liked all the Chamber's Facebook photos for you and shared them on our page too!" After taking a sip of her caramel macchiato she continued, "have you seen any new business from it?"

"Well a couple of people bought some small things on the day of, but I haven't seen the flood of new business I was hoping for last week" Eva replied.

"Take it from me, always try to link your marketing to the dollars it brings in. It can be hard and damn near impossible sometimes to do that, but the more you do it, the better you'll get at it." Marie continued, "I'm a yogi first and a business owner second. I never planned on having to worry about marketing and HR and all those damn taxes, but I'm a "get shit done" type of lady and if I was going to do it l, I was going to do it right!"

Eva laughed inwardly at Marie's candor that never got old.

"I learned the hard way on some of that stuff though."

"Like what?" Eva asked.

"Oh, it's probably stuff you already know about since you've been in marketing before."

Eva jumped in, "Well, you'd be surprised how much I don't know about all this. Marketing a small business like this is much different than marketing for a hospital chain. I mean some principles apply, but it feels much more high risk with the shop. Like how do I know what to spend our marketing dollars on? With the hospital, we had a budget we had to stick to, but whether or not the marketing actually worked or not wouldn't make or break us. People are always going to need a hospital. But with the shop, I feel like if I don't spend this marketing budget right, then it might break us."

Marie held up her coffee cup as if toasting and jokingly said "Welcome to the life of a small business owner!" They both laughed.

"Here's the thing," Marie explained, "You've got to get into the head of your best customers. Figure out where they are online and offline. Figure out what really connects with them. The way I see it, you have a few of what you marketing gurus call 'target audiences'," She continued her explanation, "You've got the kids, their parents, maybe the grandparents, and then that other crowd that likes all the books and what not." Eva, nodding in agreement, said, "Sure, that's about right." Marie continued, "Now, if you want to reach the kids, don't run an ad in the paper, or even on the tv or radio. If you want them to start begging their parents to take them to your store, throw up a commercial on YouTube.... Or even TikTok." Eva rolled her eyes in exasperation at the mention of TikTok. Marie replied to the not so subtle eye roll, "I know! I know, but it's where the kiddos are, and now even some of those kiddos have kiddos. We're getting ancient, Eva." They laughed together at the morbid humor that can only be found in the sharp awareness of one's mortality. Marie continued, "Even if you aren't doing the dances on there yourself, you can have an ad for Marley's on there."

"You can do that?" Eva asked, surprised.

"Sure! Thaxton watches YouTube non stop and I've seen commercials for the trampoline park on there." Thaxton is Marie's 10-year old son, one of the masses of pre-teens with their face stuck in a device as much as they are allowed. "And you can track the hell out of that stuff. Any advertising you do online, you can track. I use a company out of Atlanta. They got me setup so that I can see when I pay $50 for Google ads I get 2 phone calls from new potential customers. It's incredible."

"The grandparents though," Marie scrunched her face in thought, "You might be able to reach them through the newspaper, or maybe even a spot on the evening news, but for us parents, just start serving mimosas at the shop and I'm there."

On her way to the shop, Eva pondered all her options for advertising. She had never thought about targeting the kids with ads, but it made sense. How many Saturday mornings as a kid had she been glued to the television drooling over the latest and greatest toy - right in the middle of the cartoons? They didn't play those commercials during 60 Minutes, and for good reason! Traditional advertising seemed to be somewhat intuitive for her, but then she wondered if people even watch traditional broadcast television anymore. She couldn't remember the last time she had watched the nightly news. TV and radio now consisted of streaming services. "Perhaps there is a way to advertise on those!" she thought to herself.

She only knew enough about digital advertising to understand she needed to know more before making a decision. Luckily she had a meeting scheduled for the morning with Ethan at Web Monkeys to review the website before it launched. The new website was an integral step to the success of any digital ad campaign. She definitely didn't want to spend money sending people to the old Marley's site. She decided to see if they could give her any guidance to help figure out which route to go.

Advertising

An efficient marketing plan will use advertising to target people at different stages of their customer journey and should be expected to produce results at different times. In the first part of the book, we learned about a sales funnel. It helps us break down the different stages of a customer's journey - from not knowing anything about your business, to becoming a loyal customer. This concept is most relevant when you are thinking of what advertising you should invest in.

If you focus all your effort on the lower end of the sales funnel, then you will constantly be spending money (and hopefully making money) on a small group of people and never increasing the flow to that point, and thus never increasing the amount of money you are making. Spending your money on higher stages of the sales funnel helps you increase the flow of customers through the funnel.

If a local business wants to reach new customers that may or may not need them at that time, then brand awareness advertising can help them be 'top of mind' for their particular product or service. Think about car insurance. Most people don't actively shop around for car insurance for 99.999% of their lives. Most people already have it and don't think about changing providers unless there is a major event that prompts them to do so. That's why Progressive, Liberty, and Farmers' are in nearly every commercial break on TV these days. When that person does decide to change, they will most likely think of one of those companies first.

Whether or not they switch to that company is another matter. However, most people know Flo from Progressive and the "We are Farmers" jingle equally well. They are very familiar. And whether we like it or not, that familiarity makes it more likely that we will choose them. Familiarity bias or mere exposure effect, is the phenomenon that occurs when people are simply exposed to a person, thing, or brand on a regular basis. We tend to like things that are familiar to us, whether we have a real reason to or not.

Les Binet and Peter Fields also catalogue increased pricing power as another long term benefit to brand building. This means that the more people know and trust your brand, the more you can charge. We will cover pricing more later.

Billboards and radio ads (traditional or streaming) are great ways to increase brand awareness if you are a local business. They can be targeted to a certain extent: the location of a billboard might target a certain neighborhood, or business community, and a particular radio station might attract a specific demographic. The downside to non-digital brand awareness campaigns is that they tend to be expensive. Radio, billboards, and newspapers ads all come with a pretty steep price tag (and sometimes contract) compared to streaming radio, YouTube ads, or Google Display ads. This doesn't mean they aren't worth it, but if you have a limited budget, you don't want to use the lion's share on one of these because the returns are only returns if you invest long-term. Brand awareness takes time to simmer. It's the slow-cooker recipe of advertising.

Digital search ads, on the other hand, are like the microwave dinner. It doesn't take long to get an ad campaign running that starts producing results. If you've ever searched for any sort of product or service on Google, then you have most likely seen Google Search Ads. These are typically the top 2-3 results with a small 'Ad' icon next to them. If what you are searching for has local providers then you might even see an ad in the 'Map Pack'. That's the local listings below the ads with an accompanying map. While Google Search Ads can be used for top of the funnel audiences, most local businesses will benefit from using them for bottom of the funnel audiences. This means you can target those people who have already realized that they want to buy something you offer and are ready or close to ready to make a purchase decision. For instance, if you are a plumber, then running search ads against search phrases like 'plumber near me' or 'emergency plumber' would get you directly in front of people who have shown interest in your service.

The best thing about this tactic is that you only pay when they click on your ad. You can also limit how much you pay for a single click and how much you are willing to pay per day. It's important to note that the cost per click (CPC) for your business might be much different than an ad for a business in another industry. This is because your CPC is directly proportional to the amount of competition you have that is also using Google Search Ads. Google awards the best ad spots to the highest bidder. If you are in an industry that has national brands competing for clicks that are relevant to your industry, then there is a good chance that your ads will be more expensive than if your only competition is other local businesses. However, we've seen local businesses in the HVAC, plumbing, and legal fields pay a significant amount of money for their search phrases because these businesses tend to be highly competitive and can afford higher CPCs.

When the CPC begins to get too high for it to make sense as a lower funnel tactic, you might ask yourself if it's worth continuing to outbid competitors for the dual purposes of brand awareness and keeping clicks/business away from competitors. If it's not, then reduce your maximum CPC to something that makes more sense for your business.

You can also reach people in the middle of the funnel with both digital and traditional advertising tactics. These are typically people who are researching a product or service. It could be that person that just turned 40 and is batting around the idea of purchasing a motorcycle. They might be browsing listings on Facebook Marketplace, researching safety gear, etc. They aren't ready to make a decision, but they are ready for you to make an impression on them. It could be kids or parents trying to figure out what they want (or what they want to buy) for Christmas presents. In both cases, there are ways to get your brand and product or service in front of them online and offline.

In the latter case, a spread in the newspaper or a specially mailed catalog is a way for you to keep your brand and offerings in front of them as they research what they want, make their list, and check it twice. Google also uses all its data collection to help you target people mid-funnel with 'in-market audiences'. These are groups of users that Google has identified are in the market for your particular product or service. You can leverage this data for search ads or for Google Display Ads. Display ads are visual ads that you see on most websites (other than the large social media platforms) as well as in apps. They are the Home Depot ads that follow you around the internet after you look at a saw on their website. Are they kind of annoying and creepy? Yes. Are they effective? Without a doubt.

For more in-depth resources about digital ads scan the QR code below (theclimb.guide/ads)

Facebook, Instagram, Pinterest, Bing, and other platforms all offer digital advertising solutions that you can configure to reach people at different levels of the funnel to help push them to become loyal customers. For local businesses, it's not efficient or great planning to rely on just one of these tactics. The right combination is going to be different for every business, and investing in 3-4 different options helps you build your business for the long-term.

In The Long and Short of It, Les Binet and Peter Field provide a comprehensive analysis of 996 advertising campaigns and found that the most effective marketing campaigns had a 60:40 split between higher funnel, brand awareness, and lower funnel performance tactics. They also found that brands that grow, must increase their share of voice (SOV). Your share of voice is a way to think about how often your brand is in front of your customers compared to your competitors. To simplify it, think of it this way: if you have one billboard and one of your competitors has one, and the leading competitor has two, then you currently have 25% of the share of voice. If you want to grow beyond your smaller competitor, you will need to get a second billboard. If you want to be leader in your category, then you need to have three boards total. It's important to note, however, that the increase in your market share doesn't come overnight. It takes time of consistently out advertising your competition to grow your market share.

They also found that the most effective campaigns address the entire category of buyers. A broad reach leads to broader effects compared to narrow targeting. For instance, if you are selling hybrid cars, you shouldn't just focus on people who love hybrid cars, you should advertise to anyone who might need a car. This is slightly counterintuitive, but years of research backs up the importance of building your brand broadly rather than targeting a very niche market. For more information and links to the research above, visit theclimb.guide/research.

While you are thinking about what type of ads will be best for your business, you also need to consider if you will manage them or if you will pay someone to manage them. Each of the digital platforms is nuanced and changes on a regular basis. It can be hard for business owners to stay abreast of important changes, monitor their campaigns and make changes as needed, as well as run their business. The larger your budget, the more likely you need someone to manage it to ensure that you aren't wasting money and it's meeting your goals.

If you are going to try and do it on your own, I would recommend investing the time to take an intro course through Udemy or Coursera and then plan on spending 1-2 hours a week per platform managing your campaigns.

Mid-funnel campaigns can be a little more tricky to set up and monitor. However pure brand awareness and lower-funnel search ads can be set up relatively easily and don't need as much constant monitoring. The key is to get them setup correctly. Paying an agency a small fee to get them set up and monitor them for the first month, with quarterly or semi-annual check-ins, is a reasonable tactic that can save you time and give you peace of mind. Just be sure that the company or person you pay to set them up knows what they are doing.

One of the most common things businesses come to us for is help getting their Google Ads corrected. We've seen businesses that have paid a lot of money to get their Google Ads setup incorrectly. Not only do they pay that setup and management fee, but they also wind up wasting hundreds or thousands of dollars on poorly setup and managed campaigns. One of our clients provides IT support for other businesses. They specialize in wiring your office for internet access, making sure your computers are secure, and setting up your print server. They didn't feel like they were getting a lot out of their Google Ads campaigns. The phone just wasn't ringing enough for the amount of money they were using. You can imagine their surprise when I told them that they were spending hundreds of dollars a month for their ads to show up when someone searched "PlayStation Support". Ad platforms will gladly take your money, even if you're wasting it. Make sure the agency or freelancer you pay for this has a proven track record. You might also check to see if they have certifications from the ads platforms themselves. Facebook offers Blueprint certification, Google has various levels of certification, etc.

With traditional ads, it's a little easier to get them running and keep them going. Newspaper ads have been nearly the same since the beginning. The risk with traditional ads is your ability to measure their effectiveness. It's a good idea to not expect a whole lot of immediate, direct results from traditional media ads unless you are running a great sale or limited time offer. But keeping an eye on the trends of your business can help you observe their effectiveness or ineffectiveness from a bird's eye view. If your foot traffic, calls, branded searches (people searching for you by name), and buzz in the community are on an upward trend, then you might be able to credit those ad campaigns. However, if you are going to run traditional media ads, be willing to do it in force and commit to 6 months to a year.

Think about it like a pressure washer. The pressure washer is only going to be as effective as the flow of water it's getting from the water hose. If you don't turn the water hose on all the way, you're just going to waste a lot of water and make a mess. If you don't have the budget to do that then build up your business with targeted digital advertising first.

When she showed up at the Web Monkeys office the next morning, Ethan and Chloe greeted her, excited to show her the finished website. They walked her through all the pages, ensuring the content was all correct. Earlier in the process they had arranged access to Eva's domain name management account so that they could switch her hosting away from Webcorp and to Web Monkeys. "Let's get this baby launched!" Chloe said as she logged into the domain name registrar and changed the IP address to her domain's A record.

After waiting a few minutes, they refreshed marleystoysandbooks.com and Eva saw the culmination of her branding and design efforts on the screen. In that moment, it felt like the wind was at her back and she was ready to run the marathon that was ahead of her still.

Motivated by seeing the new website, Eva jumped into questions that had been rolling around in her head since last night. "The site looks amazing!" she said gratefully. "Now how do we get people there? And more importantly, how do we get them into my door?"

Ethan walked Eva through a potential customer journey for Marley's and emphasized the need to have tactics and resources that reach people at each stage of the journey. He used their whiteboard to sketch out the sales funnel and began writing in some potential tactics and budgets for each level.

Eva snapped a picture of the whiteboard with her phone to review later, thanked Ethan and Chloe for all their help and left with an heir of elation and empowerment. She felt like she could now make an educated decision about her advertising. She was looking forward to meeting with Rodney and Stephanie the next day.

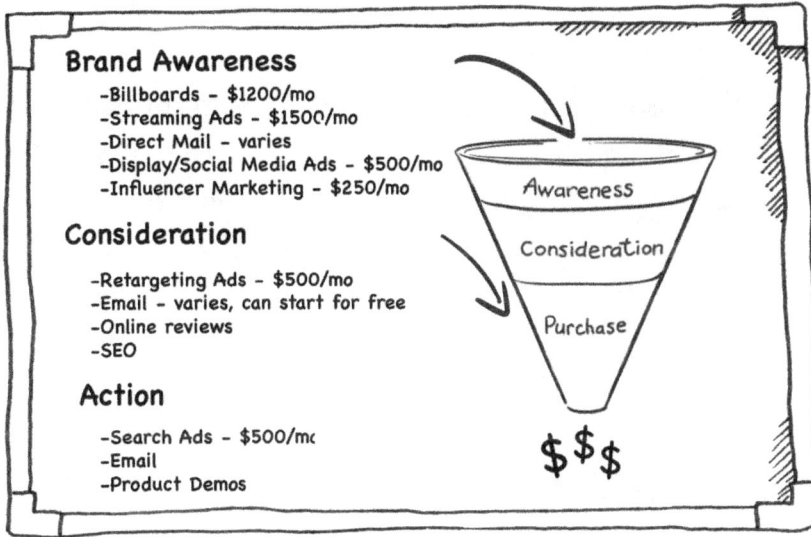

Brand Awareness
- Billboards - $1200/mo
- Streaming Ads - $1500/mo
- Direct Mail - varies
- Display/Social Media Ads - $500/mo
- Influencer Marketing - $250/mo

Consideration
- Retargeting Ads - $500/mo
- Email - varies, can start for free
- Online reviews
- SEO

Action
- Search Ads - $500/mo
- Email
- Product Demos

Awareness

Consideration

Purchase

$$$

Rodney showed up at the shop dressed in khakis, a button down, and tie. By Eva's estimation he was slightly north of 50 and carried himself as if he'd sold more than his share of ads to local businesses. He introduced himself, shaking Eva's hand firmly and asked her how business was going so far. "So far so good!," Eva replied. "We've had a great turnout from the community, but now I am trying to figure out how to get them coming back and buying more."

Rodney smiled and said, "Well, let's see if we can put something together to make that happen!" He began by asking her what her budget was and she admitted that she wasn't quite sure of what it should be. Rodney pulled out a sample newspaper from his folder and started showing her examples of what certain sizes and types of ads looked like.

She politely interrupted him and asked him about the newspaper's readers. "I am fairly certain of the strategy I want to take. I am just trying to find the right tactics that match it. Can you tell me what type of person reads your paper? Who will I be reaching if I place an ad in it?"

Rodney gave an unexpected smile and replied, "I'm glad you asked!" He continued, "I'm sure you've heard that the newspaper industry is struggling, and well, it is... but the Burlington Gazette is hanging on to try to stay independent and not get swallowed up by one of those corporations like what happened to the Willow Creek city paper. A corporation from Atlanta bought them up, fired half the staff, reduced the print frequency, and raised the ad prices. We believe in good local journalism and helping our local economy thrive and we're going to fight for it."

Eva liked where he was going with this and felt a sense of pride for her town's underdog local newspaper. "Last year we hired this data wiz. She started out as an intern, but our editor saw a lot of potential with what we can do with it. She's been helping us keep track of who reads the print, the digital, how old they are, where they live, all that. We've even been able to keep track of what articles are the most interesting to them on the website!"

As he told her about their analytics magician, his eyes lit up. This stuff was like a secret weapon for sales. "I tell you what, tell me what your goals and strategy are, who you want to reach, and I will get you some numbers and we can see if the Burlington Gazette can help you build the Marley's empire."

"That sounds like a fantastic plan!" she replied. She told him that she was interested in reaching either parents or grandparents and she was considering doing some sort of event to target one or both of those groups at the shop. "I might consider running some sort of coupon or discount occasionally to see if I can get some idea of who is actually noticing the ad."

He jotted these things down in his notebook and told her he'd send her an email before the week was out with some options. As he packed up to leave he added, "Oh! I almost forgot. Certain print ads come with complimentary ads on our website. We are still working on getting a reporting system in place so you can see how many people view and click on your ads in real time. Until then, we are just including them in the print ads."

He paused and a look of concern came across his eyes. "I don't like to speak ill of anyone, even our competition, but I hate to see Burlington businesses hurt." He continued, "At some point, someone from the daily paper in Willow Creek will probably try to get your business. Now, they have a lot of readers and their print ads might be worth a shot, but they make most of their money selling digital ads, and I've heard from more than a few of our clients that they've been burnt by them."

Surprised to get insider information like this from a sales meeting, Eva replied with her usual charm "Oh, thank you for the warning. I'll be sure to give them a harder time than I gave you."

Her lightheartedness eased the seriousness a little and Rodney smiled and finished with, "Well, I think they outsource their digital stuff to another large corporation so you never get to actually talk with people that are working on your ads. If I am paying someone that sort of money I want to be able to look them in the eye, or at least be able to talk with them on the phone!"

After they shook hands and said their goodbyes, Eva was encouraged by the direction the local paper seemed to be taking and also slightly proud that she was able to keep a sales meeting to under 15 minutes.

Eva began to pick up some scattered blocks and other toys in the demo area. She was getting used to this area being in disarray. It was a good sign. It meant more kids were coming in and playing with the toys. She had a sense that foot traffic had increased over the last month since she had started posting more on social media, but she knew better than to simply go off her gut with numbers. After she put the last train car back on the train table, she grabbed a notepad from behind the counter and started tallying up the number of people that had come through the doors on the last day. She had one column for adults and one for children. She also added an item on her to-do list, "Find a better way to track foot traffic".

She heard the bell of the front door ring and Stephanie greeted her with a big smile and an outstretched hand. Time for round two!

Stephanie's presentation wasn't as convincing as Rodney's, but she learned some good information about how television advertising works and what it costs. Ultimately, it was a little out of Eva's price range for the time being. Stephanie had also given her a presentation on the digital advertising that the station offered. It seemed impressive, so she asked if WBBB did it in house or outsourced it like the Willow Creek newspaper did. Stephanie told her it was outsourced to a large firm that was an expert in digital advertising. She wanted to weigh all her options, so she gave Stephanie some details about what she'd like to accomplish and Stephanie promised to get her some numbers asap. After Stephanie left, Eva finished the tasks for opening the shop and found a pad of paper and tried to layout a plan for her advertising while it was still fresh on her mind and she used some ball park prices from her conversions with Ethan, Rodney, and Stephanie. She jotted down a few numbers at the top:

- *$2500* (what she had left over from her dad's loan)

- *$2400* (what she would have in her budget until the end of the year since she cancelled the WebCorp subscription)

There were also a few numbers she knew would need to be included in her marketing budget every month:

- *$25 - web hosting*

- *$50 - email marketing service*

She wrote down all the months between then and the end of the year. She knew she would need more around the holiday season, but she didn't want to save it all until then. She knew that to meet her goals, she'd need to start building her brand now. As she thought threw how to split up her budget she kept in mind the 60:40 rule that Ethan had recommended to her: use 60% of the budget on long term brand building and 40% on lower funnel action.

She knew most of the long term brand building tactics like billboards and TV ads wouldn't fit in a budget of $4,900 over 6 months, so she considered some other sources. Facebook ads seemed safe, but she wasn't really sure how effective they would be. Influencer marketing seemed scary, but she knew that there were a few influential Instagram moms in her area. What if she reached out to them and asked them to feature the shop in some reels, she pondered, allowing herself to think outside of the box to make her budget work. If she were to spend $550 in July through September, she would dedicate $275 to brand awareness, $200 to lower funnel tactics like search ads, and $75 for her web hosting and email software. That would give her $3,250 to use during October and the holiday season.

- *July - September:*
  - $275 - 2 influencers?
  - $200 - search ads
  - Social Media
  - Networking at Chamber events
  - $25 - web hosting
  - $50 - email marketing
- *October - December:*
  - $300 - 2 influencers
  - $375 - Social media ads
  - $300 - Search ads
  - Social Media
  - Networking at Chamber events
  - $25 - web hosting
  - $50 - email marketing

Eva looked at the rough outline of a budget and felt that sense of accomplishment and ease that comes with completing a critical yet overdue task. She didn't know if she had budgeted enough for influencers and there were many other unknowns leading into her first holiday season.

She knew she would need to be flexible and nimble.

CHAPTER 10: MARKETING TO HUMANS

If your ad creative isn't worth remembering, then all your advertising dollars are being thrown away.

You've probably heard the truism that states that someone has to see or hear your brand 7 times before they remember it. This number often gets increased to 20, 30, or more for our modern media saturated culture, but the idea is the same: if you want people to remember your brand, then get your logo in front of them as many times as possible until its downright annoying. The problem is, that number most likely was based on the average, dull ads that have been prevalent since advertising began. It doesn't give us any insight on how to create better advertising, it just tells us that we have to put more and more money behind bad advertising to get any return out of it.

Think about your the last commercial that really made you laugh. How many times did you have to see that ad before you remembered it? Chances are once, maybe twice before you remembered the brand it it was new to you. I am a big fan of Liquid Death's branding and advertising. It's edgy and over the top. I could probably describe most of their ads in detail, because they earned a spot in my memory.

Martin Boase, former head of Omnicom UK, was quoted as saying,

"We believe that if you're going to invite yourself into someone's living room for thirty seconds, you have a duty not to bore them or insult them by shouting at them. On the other hand, if you can make them smile, or show them something interesting or enjoyable - if you're a charming guest - then they may lie you a bit better, and they may be a little more likely to buy your product" (The Anatomy of Humbug, 2015)

People behave in irrational ways. They make buying decisions in irrational ways too. And it's actually a very rational behavior that we have developed. Think about it this way: we are exposed to thousands of ads every day, from jingles on the radio, to billboards, to logos on cars as we drive from point A to point B. I challenge you to count the number of brands you see or hear on your way to work tomorrow. You will probably tire of the exercise before you get to the office. We also have 101 stressors in our lives - what time is my kid's band concert tonight, am I supposed to take them, did John call client XYZ yesterday like he was supposed to, did my spouse pay the electric bill, is it due today? With all this going on, it's mentally impossible to process and analyze our way through all things we encounter in our lives day in and day out, not to mention analyze why we buy or don't buy a particular brand of shampoo. This is due partly to the biology of our brain. When we are deep in thought and using the analytical portion of our brain, it uses more glucose. Evolution has trained our brains to use less glucose as a matter of survival, and in turn we have developed shortcuts, or what Daniel Khaneman in his foundational book, "*Thinking Fast and Slow,*" calls heuristics (pronounced 'hyoo-RIS-tiks'). Khaneman and his research partner, Amos Tversky, developed the concept of System 1 and System 2 thinking. System 1 kicks in when our evolved brain is able to use shortcuts to make a decision. The difference between the two systems can be demonstrated with a simple math quiz:

$1 + 1 = ?$

$2 + 7 = ?$

$1032 \times 517 = ?$

You could answer questions like #1 and 2 all day long and feel like a rockstar because your brain would be utilizing System 1 to help you answer them as quickly as possible. Question 3, however, makes you shift your mind into a different gear. It starts using more glucose, you have to do longer calculations. This is System 2.

Below are some of the common ways we do this. Khaneman and Tversky identified several biases and heuristics that you can leverage in your marketing.

Availability Heuristic

You are in a rush at the grocery store, we need to pick up something for a recipe that we are unfamiliar with. The various options of that product all look foreign to us. New names, new brands, etc. However, we see one option that is made by a brand we've used before for other products, so we grab that one. This is called the Availability Heuristic and we use it to simplify complex situations.

Anchoring Heuristic

Or consider this scenario, you go to a new restaurant for a special occasion in order to impress your date. You scan the menu and see prices that make you reconsider your career choices. The first price on the entree section is Prime Rib (along with some sauces and sides you're not sure how to pronounce). You look over to the right and see the price at $59. You quickly look to the next item and to your relief, you see that one of the steak options is at $42 and the chicken is the low, low price of $27. Whether you knew it or not, the restaurant might not even want you to get the prime rib, they are using it as the anchor price. Our brains see the first price and judge all the prices based off of it. When you see $27 for a chicken dinner, you don't compare it to the $17 price at your favorite restaurant, you see it as less than half of the prime rib. This is called the anchoring heuristic.

A practical example of how this might be applied in Marley's might happen if Eva had a new large toy that she didn't expect to sell many of, she could use it as anchor for when people came into the store. It could be displayed prominently and perhaps marked up an additional 10% so that the other prices on products around it looked more attractive.

Representative Heuristic

The representative heuristic is when we judge one thing or even a person based on what we know or have experienced with other things or people that look similar to them, often ignoring statistical realities. It's why we automatically see someone with studious-looking glasses and assume they are smart, or someone with a sweater tied around their shoulders and assume they probably drive a better car than we do.

Familiarity Bias:

Familiarity bias, or mere exposure effect, can be very powerful in brand awareness advertising, as we discussed in the last chapter. Simply by seeing a brand name and becoming familiar with it, makes it easier for a person to choose it, with no other rational reason to support that choice. The University of Michigan conducted a study that demonstrates this effect. In their student newspaper they printed an ad-like box on the front page of the paper which contained one of the following Turkish-sounding words: *kadirga, saricik, biwonjni, nansoman,* and *iktitaf.* These words appeared in varying frequencies. Some appeared more, some less. When the ads ended, the researchers sent questionnaires out across the university that asked people whether the words meant something good or something bad. The words that appeared more frequently were rated as much more favorable than the words that appeared less frequent.

To make this effect even more interesting, the effect works even when images or words are shown so fast that the conscious brain cannot interpret them, demonstrating that System 1 can respond to events that System 2 is not even aware of.

If you'd like to dive deeper into the world of behavioral economics, scan this QR Code or visit theclimb.guide/irrational

There are several more heuristics and biases that can be leverage in your marketing. It is my hope with this section to pique your curiosity enough so that you begin to think about your marketing a little more irrationally.

The wild thing about our heuristics and biases is that even when we know they exist, we can't just flip a switch and pretend they don't. They still affect our decisions and feelings. However, with time, we can train our brains to be less affected by them.

So, why does this matter and why am I writing about it?

Because people make irrational buying decisions and fortunately or unfortunately, you are relying on those irrational decisions to grow your business. So, leaning into them can help you influence their decision to buy from you. If you think back to our customer journey map, consider all those touch points.

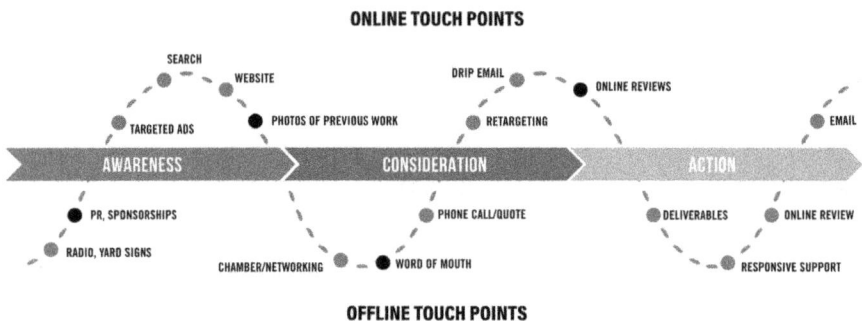

ONLINE TOUCH POINTS

SEARCH
WEBSITE
DRIP EMAIL
ONLINE REVIEWS

TARGETED ADS
PHOTOS OF PREVIOUS WORK
RETARGETING
EMAIL

AWARENESS
CONSIDERATION
ACTION

PR, SPONSORSHIPS
PHONE CALL/QUOTE
DELIVERABLES
ONLINE REVIEW

RADIO, YARD SIGNS
CHAMBER/NETWORKING
WORD OF MOUTH
RESPONSIVE SUPPORT

OFFLINE TOUCH POINTS

When you leverage knowledge about how humans think and make decisions it can be like super charging those touch points so that it nudges people a little faster through that journey.

There is a good chance, if you have been in business for any amount of time, that you've attempted some sort of marketing campaign, sure that it would cause people to come running through your door or leave your phone ringing off the hook. It might have been clever, timely, priced right. It may have had all the right elements that would make a rational person swoon over your product, but a week after launching the campaign, you saw no significant increase in business. The assumption we all make at some point is that people are making rational decisions about business. People are not hooked by our bullet pointed lists of differentiation. People are hooked by irrational emotion. And if you can get them hooked, they will take the time to read and digest your bullet points. As advertising great David Ogilvy says, "You cannot bore people into buying your product; you can only interest them in buying it."

I am going to make an assumption that in your pocket or on your desk is either an Apple iPhone or some sort of Android powered mobile phone. I am also going to assume that you are to some degree or another loyal to that brand and have many reasons why your brand is better than the other brand. The reality is they both do pretty much the same thing, but in slightly different ways. And if you're honest, you didn't choose the brand you have because of all those things, but after you chose your brand, you had enough interest to learn all the things and read the bullet pointed lists.

Your customers are the same way with your brand, each and every one of your competitors has a bullet pointed list of why they are better than everyone else. The winner will be the one that can capture customers on an irrational level.

Orlando Wood, in his book Lemon, details how the effectiveness of advertising has consistently declined over the last 15 years or so. This is in large part due to the fact that the advertisements themselves have shifted away from system 1 and more towards system 2. This shift has been made in part because the culture at large has shifted towards more a left-brained, flat way of looking at the world and ads have followed suit. However, his research along with others demonstrate that effective advertising still relies heavily on whether or not it can appeal to a person's system 1 thinking.

"Feeling happens before thinking, is evolutionarily older, and more strongly associated with motivation... So a marketer's goal is not to increase consideration, as is commonly thought, but to reduce it; to make decisions-making as quick and intuitive for people as possible."

The best way to connect with your audience is humor. If you can make someone laugh, they will remember your ad. They may even tell their friends about it. And while it is the best, it is also the hardest.

Pricing, Promotions, and Perception! Oh My!

Imagine this scenario: You have 1000 customers that are on a recurring monthly subscription for your service or product and they pay on average $25. Your COGS increases and you need to make a $2000 difference month to month. One option is to increase your customer base to 1080. For most businesses, a 10% increase in a month's time is pretty drastic. Your other option might be to increase the price of your service to $26.99. A $1.99 increase would be perceived as significantly less than $2 by your customers, and as long you don't have increases on a regular basis, they should be able to absorb it without too much fuss.

Obviously, this scenario has been simplified, but the point is that how you price things can affect your business drastically.

Now imagine that instead of $26.99, you raised the price to $27. It's just a penny more and it will help people manage their checking accounts a little easier. What you might not expect is that people would see this price as significantly higher than $26.99.

I could get into the weeds about why this happens, but instead I will leave you with some key points to observe when considering your pricing:

- When bundling products, present the under-performing product as free.

- Do not discount luxury items.

- When negotiating a sell of a higher priced product or service, customers will see more precise pricing as more justified.

- How you present discounts visually matters.

- If a discount is less than $100 use the percentage. If it is over $100, use the dollar amount (10% off $10 is better than $1 off).

These are the tip of the proverbial iceberg however. I encourage you to grab a copy of Handbook on the Psychology of Pricing as it catalogues every major study on pricing to date.

As you determine the pricing for your products or services, don't be scared to experiment. You probably won't get it right on the first try, and that's OK. It took us five tries to get one of our core services priced optimally, and we might change it again in the near future. If you don't change your pricing from time to time, you will never know if you are pricing things optimally or not. And as in everything related to marketing and sales, measure and track it as much as possible.

I have had the opportunity to teach a business foundations course for our local entrepreneur center. One of the most common hurdles I have seen young businesses struggle with is pricing. More often than not, they undervalue their product or service. It can be a mental hurdle to overcome a false sense of humility and charge a price that's fair... to you! The only way you can have the best business possible, is for you to charge as much as the market will bear for your services. Again, there is a line that if you cross it, you will lose more sales than you are making, but don't be afraid to test where that line is. You owe it to yourself, your employees, and your community to be a thriving business.

Pitfall Warning:

Watch out for discounts. Many people assume that a great way to 'get people in the door' is to offer discounts. However, studies have shown that brands that offer discounts don't gain new customers. They simply get less money from existing customers who were happy to pay full price. When you are considering a price promotion, recalculate it as a marketing cost and see if you could ultimately make more money and build your brand by using those dollars to advertise rather than discount. For instance, if you were going to give a $15 discount on a $100 product and you expected to sell a total of 100 of them, with the discount bringing 50 of those purchases, then you are dedicating $1500 to that discount. If you were to use that $1500 on better ads or marketing, could you bring in 50 or more additional sales while also building your brand?

CHAPTER 11: THE SEO MOUNTAIN

Priority: Varies
Customer Journey: All

When Eva got to the shop the next morning, her dad was already there, tidying up. "Do you know what today is?" he asked with a child like glee.

With a suspicious look in her eyes, she replied, "No... what day is it?"

"Today is the day that Shadow Stalkers announce their next big product!" For an old man, his ability to stay informed of news that usually only interests teenagers impressed her.

"That's exciting!" she said, attempting to echo his level of enthusiasm.

"They should be having a press conference or something at noon," he explained. "We should check it out and call our supplier right away about getting some once we know the details. Maybe even have Chris make some of those TikToks for it."

That wasn't a half bad idea, she thought to herself. "OK, but only if you do that dance he was trying to get you to do for one last week," she goaded him.

"Tik Tok is not ready for Eugene Marley!" he declared jokingly as he emptied his dust pan in the trash.

The day turned out to be pretty steady. When it slowed down around noon she went in the back to find her dad at the computer Googling "cool product" in search for the much-anticipated product reveal news. "Hey, when I google "cool product" why doesn't our shop come up? When people start googling that, we could get a lot of business if our shop was at the top. Will our new website do that?"

"I don't think that's how it works dad", she said, half joking, half uncertain. His question sparked a barrage of questions in her mind. If people could find Marley's through Google without her paying for ads, then that could be a game changer! How do they get on Google, what would people search for to find them, who would be searching? She remembered her conversation with Ethan about how they didn't guarantee search results. She didn't think much of it at the time, but now that she saw the potential in them, she wanted to find out more.

She sent Ethan a quick email from her phone, "Do you have time to talk today? I have a few SEO questions."

Just then her dad exclaimed, "Found it!"

She turned around to see a YouTube live video playing with the CEO of Shadow Stalkers standing on stage next to pedestal with a figurine clad in a rugged, dark leather ensemble, equipped for the perils of monster hunting. The attire is accentuated with metallic armor pieces at the shoulders and knees, providing a balance between agility and protection on it. The figure's face was hidden beneath a leather hood.

She started to ask, "Is that the new..."

"It's Aurora Nightshade, her cloak and hood is made out of real vegan leather!" her father excitedly interrupted her. "It's going to be a big seller this year!" While Eva was perfecting the business side of the toy shop, she realized she still had a lot to learn about the toy side of the business.

Her phone dinged. It was Ethan's reply. "Sure do! Come by anytime."

"I'll be right back, Dad," Eva said, as she grabbed her coat and headed out the door.

"See ya later alligator," he replied, without looking away from the press conference on the screen.

Eva entered the Web Monkey's office as Ethan was getting a refill at the coffee pot. "Hey there! That was quick!" Ethan remarked. "Want some coffee?" he offered.

"No thanks, but I am interested in some of those Google search rankings we had talked about early on." She said, "But before we get into that, let me just say, I keep getting compliments on the new website! You took our brand and made it come to life! I am starting to understand what you were talking about now."

"That's great to hear! Now, these SEO questions. They seem urgent. What's up?" Ethan asked before taking a sip of his coffee?

Eva explained to him her thought of bypassing paid ads in favor of, what she would learn are called, 'organic results'. Organic results are the non-paid search engine results. Ethan nodded as she explained her idea and ended with the question, "So, how do we get to the top of those results?"

"Let's take a look at what you're talking about in the wild," he said, leading her to his desk where they could both see his screen. He opened up a browser and asked her, "What do you want to be found for?"

She told him about the new product, "I want to be found when people search for Shadow Stalkers." He typed in 'Shadow Stalkers' to the search bar, and within a few seconds his browser was populated with links, images, and even some videos.

"The world of search engine optimization is pretty complex, and anyone who says they understand it all and can guarantee anything is either lying to you or themselves. Google is a black box, that I'm not even sure the people at Google understand exactly how it delivers results."

"However," he continued, "there are a few guiding principles and things to know about SEO. The first and most important thing to recognize as a local business is that there are really two types of search engine optimization worlds. The first and biggest is just SEO in general. I like to call it 'national SEO', because most of the time you are competing for the rankings with sites all across the nation and sometimes internationally. This applies to things that aren't geographically bound. For instance 'best computer this year' would get you results from all over the world and it wouldn't matter where those sites are based out of because their location isn't relevant to the answer you are looking for. The best computer this year is theoretically the same, whether you are in New York or LA."

Eva nodded along and was taking mental notes as he explained further, "The same applies to other generalized searches, 'apple pie recipe', 'how to train my dog', etc. These are going to deliver results from all over. And if you are going to try to rank for one of these searches, you will have to compete with other sites all over the world."

"The second type of SEO is Local SEO." Eva began to wonder if she should take out a pen and paper at this point and hoped there wouldn't be a quiz later. Ethan continued, "This refers to the results that Google or Bing give you based on where you are located or the location you are searching for. These types of searches will typically give you what we in the industry call the 'map pack'. It's the handful of listings with the map near the top of the search results. Google has identified certain searches as local by default. Searches like 'plumbers', 'grocery stores', or 'therapists' are going to default to local results. Other searches can toggle between national and local search results depending on if there is a geographic location in the search itself 'iPhones near me' or 'computers in Burlington' would most likely deliver local cell phone or computer stores in our area at the top."

If it weren't for the pressing nature of her question, Ethan may have lost her attention by now, but she felt these questions were urgent for her business, and rightly so. She was quickly running through the options for national versus local searches for Marley's as Ethan continued "For your search, Google hasn't quite identified mythical monster hunters as a local category, so if you want to get to the top of that search specifically, then you'll be competing with all these other sites that have been working hard to get there."

Ethan saw a little bit of disappointment in Eva's face, so he reassured her, "Don't worry though. If you want to be found locally for national searches, you can use search ads - like we talked about last time. I can explain that more in a bit, but first I want to finish your crash course in SEO".

Eva perked up a little, "Great! Keep going!"

How SEO Works

SEO, or search engine optimization, is consistently one of the most misunderstood marketing tactics for small business owners. Getting to the top of the page for a desired search phrase is theoretically science, but it seems like magic. What works, what doesn't, and why? We might not ever know all the answers to those questions, but we do know some of the guiding principles. Disclaimer: those guiding principles have changed in the past and will most likely change in the future, making SEO a never-ending battle of king of the hill. I am going to approach this topic with Google as the primary search engine since 92% of users search with Google. For comparison, Bing comes in a distant second place at 3%.

- Principle #1:
  - Google wants to serve the best and most helpful results to its users.
- Principle #2

- o   If you try to manipulate the results, you will get penalized at some point.
- Principle #3:
- o   Refer to Principle #1.

Google wants to serve the best and most helpful results to its users. This is how Google keeps people coming back. If it starts serving results that aren't helpful, then people will stop using it. So, the real question is, how do you send Google the right signals to help it understand that your site is the best result for the searches you are targeting?

From a general SEO perspective there are more factors that can be tweaked and fine-tuned to help you systematically achieve better results compared to local SEO. These include keyword density, the overall authority of your site, the authority and quantity of links to your site (and the target page in particular), inner-site linking, the amount of time people spend on your site after clicking on your link in the search results, and whether or not they return to Google and search more after they click on your site. Some things that are important for both general and local SEO are:

- Page speed

- Mobile optimization

- Authoritative links coming into your site

- The amount of time someone spends on your site once they get there from a search result

You may hear of SEO 'silver bullets' from time to time. Things like having a YouTube video on your landing page, making sure you have exact search phrases used in a particular way, etc. These things can be helpful to try, but don't set your expectations high. Google changes the relevance of these elements on a regular basis. If you operate a nationwide business that has the ability to convert web traffic into customers independent of geography, then it might make sense to invest the time and resources needed to rank in the top 10 of Google.

Local SEO

As a reminder, local SEO is relevant to searches that Google associates with local businesses. The results for these searches will often have what is called a 'map pack', or 3-4 local listings accompanied by a map of the search area. If you can make it into these top listings, you get some additional perks that regular listings don't get including your Google review rating displayed, along with your phone number, address, and website. Google uses a few factors to determine if you are looking for a local business, such as:

- A city or region in your search phrase. "Best Italian Restaurant in Washington DC"

- The phrase "near me"

Or if it has previously determined the phrase you are searching for is most likely meant to be a local business, it will default to local searches. There are some categories of businesses that Google has learned are almost always tied to local searches. So, if you Google "plumbers", for instance, you don't need to put 'near me' or a city with it. Google will automatically serve you local results.

There are certain elements that are extremely important for local SEO results. One of the highest is your Google Review quantity and quality (more on this in the next section). Google sees this as a clear signal that people think you're great (remember, their main objective is to serve the best results, so this helps). The added bonus for having a lot of great reviews is that if you make it into the top 3 results, people will more naturally click on you over your competitor if you have more and better results than they do, even if you're not #1 in the list. Second on the list for local SEO is the consistency of your name, address, and phone number across the internet. If your name, address, and phone number (or NAP) is inconsistent, then it's a signal to Google that you aren't taking the time to maintain your online presence. It might seem arbitrary, but it's one of the known signals to Google that they have confirmed is used in local search result rankings. Does your NAP on your website and social media match your Google Business Profile (formerly Google My Business). There are also several other lower-importance sources that Google uses to determine NAP consistency. You can check yours at the QR code below.

Find more details about SEO, local SEO, and Google Business Profile by scanning the QR code or visiting theclimb.guide/seo

Many times, business owners will focus on their website for local SEO and forget they also have a source for this data on Google directly with their Google Business Profile. This is where you get to tell Google directly what your business does, when they're open, where it's located, and more. Making sure your Google Business Profile is set up and optimized is an important factor in your local search rankings.

When Eva got back to her car after her meeting with Ethan, she quickly jotted down a to-do list of things she needed to improve to help her local SEO:

- Better/More Reviews

- Google Business Profile optimization

- NAP consistency

She was leaning on Ethan and the Web Monkeys team to make sure her site was fast, mobile optimized, and accessible.

CHAPTER 12: HELPING GOOGLE LIKE YOU

Risk: Low
Reward: Medium
Customer Journey: Consideration and Action

Eva began implementing her advertising campaign in August and now fall was right around the corner. Pressure was building for holiday season sales. And like many other retailers, Marley's relied on holiday shopping to bring in the highest volume of traffic, inventory, and sales for the year. For the last 3 months, the shop had been scraping by. The new branding had helped revive interest from the locals, but she knew that at this pace she wasn't going to meet her holiday goals. She knew that the holiday season would give her the best opportunity to springboard into the new year and meet the overall goals she had set in early summer. Online reviews seemed like a good low hanging fruit to start with.

Over the last few months Marley's was able to rack a few new Google reviews. They now had five 5 star reviews. There weren't many, but it's a start, thought Eva. Just for comparison's sake, she Googled 'toy stores atlanta' and 'toy stores charlotte'. The top results hovered around the 50-70 count, with one outlier in

Charlotte with nearly 400. 5 reviews. It's... a start, she reminded herself. She remembered what Ethan had told her. "You don't have to ask for negative reviews, those carry their own energy. You have to prompt people for a great review." She felt it might be awkward to ask customers to leave a review as they left the store. There must be a good way to do it. In the meantime, she had several friends who had bought something since the grand reopening. They were the 'low hanging fruit'. She estimated she could bump her count past 10 reviews with a few friendly texts. She would drop the link to her Google Business Profile directly in the text and make it incredibly easy for her friends to help her out. Now she just had to get a link to her Google Business Profile!

She searched 'Marley's Home for Wayward Books and Gifted Toys". The first listing appeared with an old image of the exterior of the shop and the address. The name on the listing read "Marley's Toys and Books", the old name. Eva searched the page for a little pencil icon she had come to recognize as the edit link. It was nowhere to be found. Then she spotted a little link under the images and address. "Own this business?" "Heck yeah I do!", she said to herself as she clicked the link. After a few more clicks, Eva came to a screen that requested a verification. Google was going to send her a postcard to the shop's address and she would have to enter the code on it before they would give her access to her profile. She was at once frustrated by the delay, but also thankful that some random person couldn't get access to her page.

Google Business Profile

Creating and optimizing a Google Business Profile (GBP), formerly known as Google My Business, is a crucial step for any business looking to improve its online presence and local SEO. Here's a comprehensive guide on how to do this effectively:

- Create or Claim Your Business Profile:

  - If your business isn't already listed on Google, create a new Google Business Profile. If it's already listed, claim it. This process involves verifying your business through a phone call or postcard from Google.

- Provide Accurate and Comprehensive Information:

  - Ensure all business details are accurate: your business name, address, phone number, and website. This information should be consistent across all online platforms.

  - Include a thorough description of your business, using relevant keywords that potential customers might use to find services or products like yours.

- Choose the Right Business Category:

  - Selecting the correct category is vital for Google to understand what your business offers and match it with appropriate searches.

- You can choose multiple categories, but the primary category should be the most accurate representation of your business.

- Add High-Quality Photos and Videos:

  - Upload high-quality images of your business, including the exterior, interior, team members, and products or services.

  - Regularly update photos to keep your profile fresh and engaging. Consider adding videos for a more comprehensive view of your business.

- Manage and Respond to Reviews:

  - Encourage customers to leave reviews on your GBP.

  - Respond promptly and professionally to all reviews, whether positive or negative. This shows that you value customer feedback and are attentive to client needs.

- Utilize the Posts Feature:

  - Use the posts feature to update customers about news, offers, events, and new products or services.

  - Regular posts can increase engagement and keep your business relevant in search results.

- Update Business Hours Regularly:

  - Keep your business hours up to date, especially during holidays or special events.

  - Accurate hours ensure customers know when they can visit or contact you, reducing the chance of negative experiences.

- Use Messaging Features:

- o   Enable the messaging feature in your GBP to allow customers to contact you directly through your profile.
- o   This can improve customer service and engagement.

- Add Products and Services:

  - o   List the products and services you offer, along with descriptions and prices. This helps customers know what you provide before they visit your store or website.

- Monitor GBP Insights:

  - o   Regularly check your GBP insights to understand how customers find your business and interact with your listing.
  - o   Use this data to refine your profile and strategies.

- Encourage Check-Ins and User-Generated Content:

  - o   Encourage satisfied customers to check in at your location and share their experiences.
  - o   User-generated content can act as organic endorsements for your business.

- Keep Your Profile Updated:

  - o   Regularly review and update your profile to ensure all information is current and accurate.

- Optimize for Voice Search:

  - o   Since voice search is increasingly popular, include conversational keywords and phrases in your business description and posts.

- Utilize Google's Q&A Feature:

  - o   Monitor and answer questions asked on your GBP promptly.

- o   This can be a way to provide valuable information to potential customers.

- Leverage Local SEO Strategies:

    - o   Alongside optimizing your GBP, implement broader local SEO strategies. This includes optimizing your website for local keywords, building local backlinks, and ensuring NAP (Name, Address, Phone Number) consistency across the web.

A well-optimized Google Business Profile can significantly improve your business's visibility and attract more local customers. It's a dynamic tool that should be actively managed and updated to reflect the current state and offerings of your business. Remember, GBP is often the first interaction potential customers have with your business online, so make it count!

As Eva thought through the review-request process, she realized that there wasn't a great way to request a review without gathering some sort of followup contact info from her customers. How could she legitimately gather a cell number or email? She hated giving her info out to stores when she shopped. She realized that she might not get everyone's info, but if she didn't have a system then she wouldn't get anyone's info and consequently no followup review requests. On a hunch she googled "Beanology", the local coffee shop she frequented and used for her grand re-opening. 157 reviews with an average score of 4.8. "Wow!" She thought. "I wonder what they are doing?" She remembered getting texts from them. Was one of them a review request? She decided to play detective and go to Beanology. If nothing else, it was a great excuse to get a mocha latte!

When she got up to the counter she noticed the white tablet and cash drawer system that had become a standard in coffee shops and boutiques over the last few years. The cashier gave the standard spiel, "Welcome to Beanology, what can I get you?" Eva noticed the cashier's name tag. Nicole was her name, and her title read 'manager'. Eva was in luck. "I need two things. First is a mocha latte."

"OK," the cashier said as she punched the order into the tablet, "what else?"

"Well, I am really curious about how your texting thing works. How do you know to send me a text after I order?" Nicole didn't seem to be in a super chatty mood so Eva explained, "My name is Eva. I run the toy shop around the corner and I am trying to figure out how to get more reviews."

At that Nicole's face brightened, "Oh, Marley's?"

"That's what we call it!" Eva replied.

"I love that store! I haven't had the chance to come in since the face lift, but I love getting my nephew's presents from there. So... more reviews?"

"Yes. I noticed Beanology has 157, so I figured y'all must be doing something right. Can you help me?"

"Anything for Marley's! We use a point of sale system that gets your phone number, some people type it in here, but somehow it has numbers for some of our customers. Anyways, I think it associates a debit card with their phone numbers so that whenever they buy something with that card, it sends them a text. I think we have the ability to change what the texts say and when they are sent."

"How cool is that?!" Eva replied. She got the name of the point of sale system (POS) they use so she could research it later.

"Yeah, we can use the system to set up loyalty programs too. It's pretty cool." At that, the barista placed a frothy dark brown drink on the counter and called out "Eva!" Eva thanked Nicole for her help and encouraged her to stop by the shop sometime for a 10% loyal customer discount.

Review Solicitation

Picture this, you wrap up with a customer, they laud the quality of the service they received, how everyone was so helpful and friendly, and how they will definitely be back again. Knowing that this person is a great candidate to leave you a glowing review online, you say, "Thank you so much for saying that! Since you had such a good experience, would you mind to leave us a review on Google?" The customer might respond with something like, "Of course! I would love to help." They leave, you and your team feel a renewed sense of pride in your work and you eagerly wait to get that notification from Google that your new biggest fan just left a review. Then... crickets. Who knows what happened after they walked out the door, but in reality there life has a ton of other things that are more important or more interesting than leaving you a review, so they forget or put it off only to be forgotten later.

If you haven't had this experience, then you will at some point. Getting bad reviews is easy. When people have a bad experience, they don't forget to let the world know about it. That experience carries its own energy that drives a person to leave a nasty 1 star review. Unfortunately, we have to ask (and sometimes beg) for the good reviews. No matter how good the product or service was, leaving a review about it is not most people's first reaction.

Review solicitation has become a big business in the last decade. Several platforms like Podium, Toast, and others have sprung up and allow you to easily request reviews from customers. If you have a retail or ecommerce business, you have several options to easily integrate review solicitation into your customer interactions. A typical review solicitation automation might look like this:

- A customer checks out at a point of sale system connected to Stripe or Square.

- The POS then checks to see if the customer's card is associated with an email or cell number.

- If it is, then a review request is texted or emailed to the customer with a link that takes them directly to the GBP profile to leave a review

To find some helpful resources on review solicitation, scan this QR code or visit theclimb.guide/reviews

If you do not use a POS that has those types of integrations, you can accomplish the same thing by copying and pasting a standard message to customers after they buy from you. It might look something like this:

> "Thank you for shopping at {{*your business name*}}! We hope you had a great experience. If you did, we would love to hear about it in a Google review here: {{*link to GBP review page*}}. If you didn't please respond to this text and let us know how we can improve."

The reason you want to send these requests over text is that 98% of texts are read. Sending people a text with a link to your review page cuts out several steps for them. They don't have to Google your business and find the review link. You are making it extremely easy for them. You will still need to send out several requests for each one you get, but having a process and system to do it will help you get it done.

Depending on your industry, you might want to solicit reviews for TripAdvisor, Yelp, or other niche review sites. Many of the review solicitation platforms allow you to alternate between platforms so that you can distribute reviews between them as needed.

Eva took a drink of the thick sugary caffeine boost as she walked back to the store. Marley's point of sale system wasn't much of a system at all. Just a basic cash register and drawer that could probably be a prop on Stranger Things. She knew there would be an additional cost to get something like Beanology's system going. Her marketing budget was getting thin, so she was going to have to find an affordable solution.

Later that evening, she got another notification on her phone, "Congratulations, you got a 5-star review from nicolebear95!"

CHAPTER 13: A MOUNTAIN OF EMAIL

Priority: High
Customer Journey: Consideration and Action

The next morning in the shop, the phone rang. Eva answered, "Thanks for calling Marley's Home for Wayward Books and Gifted Toys, how can I help you?"

"Is this Eva?" the voice on the other line responded.

"It is." Eva replied, "How can I help you?"

"Hey Eva, this is Bill Jackson from Shadow Stalkers."

Bill was Marley's rep with the company. Eva only knew him by hearing her father talk about him in reference to the toy company. She knew that he had always been a big fan of Marley's. Bill continued, "Eugene has told me all about you. Congrats on revamping the business. We have been rooting for you over here!"

Eva felt slightly flattered that Shadow Stalkers would know who she is or be rooting for her. "Well hello Bill, my dad has told me all about you and we've been super excited about the new Arora Nightshade action figure!"

"That's great!" Bill replied, "That's actually why I am calling. I was able to pull a few strings and get a few pallets of them held back from the big box stores in the greater Burlington area so that we can launch the product in your area from your store."

Eva was speechless. This would put them on the map regionally. It was one of those year-making moments that most small business owners would kill for. "That's amazing Bill - thank you!" she said, managing to string together something intelligible while her mind whirled around with the implications of this opportunity.

"Just consider it my consolation gift for not being at the grand re-opening." he replied. "Now, you'll need to think about how to get this info out there to your customers. It will look bad, if these things are just lingering on the shelf. Do you have an email list or anything you can send out an announcement to?"

Eva's stomach sank. She hadn't been able to find any record of email addresses that her dad had collected and all the business cards from the ribbon cutting were collecting dust in the office. "Yes," she said reluctantly, "but it's not much of one. When will they be here?" she asked, hoping she had enough time to pull something together for a promotion.

"They aren't scheduled to hit the shelves until next month. We are planning an October 31st launch date. Can you make that happen?"

Unsure if she wanted to know the answer or not, Eva asked "Exactly how many Aurora Nightshades do we have to sell to make this a success?"

"I have 200 units reserved for your store, and there are more where that came from, but we need those sold by Christmas."

Eva hoped that Bill couldn't hear the gulping noise she made when she heard that number. She knew this would be a mountain to conquer. October 31 was 8 weeks away. They would have to start planning yesterday to make sure a campaign for this would be successful, but she also knew the payoff for such an opportunity would be worth some overtime. If she could make this happen, then it had the potential to put her ahead of her overall business goals for the year.

"You better believe it Bill," she replied resolutely.

"Great! Oh and tell Eugene hi for me."

They said goodbye and Eva hung up the phone, her mind still racing with ideas for this new opportunity. Just then, the bell on the front door rang. It was her dad, carrying a white box and a huge smile. "Guess what today is!" he said, as he cheerfully strolled towards her with the box.

"Is there another Shadow Stalkers press conference today?" she replied sarcastically.

"No - it's your 3 month anniversary of owning the store!" He opened the box and presented her with a small cake with a rough icing version of Marley's logo on the top. "I'm proud of you kiddo."

She wiped a tear from her eye and looked at him, wanting to explode with the news, "Well, I have a surprise for you too! Guess who just called...."

You've probably heard the old saying "the cheapest customer to get is the one you've already got." While this saying doesn't apply in every situation, if it were ever true, it would be in relation to email marketing. For nine of the last twelve years, email has earned the #1 spot in marketing surveys regarding which tactic provides the most return on your investment (ROI).

When you are looking to achieve revenue goals, sometimes it's easier to draw from people who have already purchased from you and are likely to purchase from you again. If you have collected some sort of contact information from them, a cell number, email address, or physical address, then you can reach back out to them and get more business from them without having to run all the ads and marketing that it took to get them in the first place. Taking advantage of this 'cheapest customer' concept is best exemplified through email marketing. Email marketing is one of the only effective, free ways to get short-term results. You've already done the hard work of collecting their information. Email marketing is an example of owned media. With other avenues of marketing, another company owns the audience or the platform that you are using. When you advertise on Facebook, YouTube, or Google, you are just renting time with the audience that they built. Email marketing is different, because you own the audience.

Almost all efforts to get your brand, sale, or new product in front of people costs money. Ads, direct mail, billboards, sponsorships. You have to pay for those things every time you want people to see it whether they are brand new or have been your customers for years. Email marketing is one of the only tactics in your marketing arsenal that is free (or nearly free) and has a proven track record of returns with current or past customers. The effectiveness and potential of your email marketing relies on three things:

- The size of your email list

- The quality of your email list

- And the quality of your content

Email List Size:

In a nutshell, the more email addresses you have of your customers, the more return you will get out of email marketing. It's also important to say, the more data you have about your customers in general, the more you will get out of your email marketing. Having a system to collect your customers' names, emails, birthdays, addresses, and more can be extremely valuable to your marketing efforts. There are several ways to collect this information and can vary from industry to industry. For retail businesses, the easiest place to collect information is at the register. Simply getting a name plus phone number or email address for every customer that comes through your shop can be a game changer.

Typically, people are less likely to hand over a good email address, but sometimes you can offer incentives for doing so such as monthly specials and other perks. Home-service businesses typically need to build that data collection into their onboarding or project wrap up processes. Asking for an email address for invoices, appointment reminders, and the like is pretty common practice and consumers are less suspicious of getting salesy emails from the local plumber than they are from the department store in the mall.

The key is to find a process that you can consistently execute that is effective at gathering that information without being pushy or salesy with your customers. In some businesses, you might even have the opportunity to collect contact info from potential customers. If you are a professional services business, consider developing a downloadable resource on your website that people would 'pay' you for with their email address. If you are a retail business, there might be opportunities to collect this data from potential customers. Some of opportunities to collect potential customer contact info:

- Launching a new store or location

- A new product or service is coming soon

- Sign ups for holiday specials

- For ecommerce, you can collect info from customers when the product they want is out of stock

- A giveaway contest

- Collecting business cards at networking events

Email list quality:

The effectiveness of your email marketing is not only directly proportional to your email list size, but also your email list quality. Quality can come in various forms. The foundational metric is whether people are actually potential customers or not. If you are a retail shop and you have a lot of out of state email addresses, those probably aren't going to pay off... until you add ecommerce to your site. The next level of quality is the thoroughness of your data. Do you simply have an email address or do you have all the other info that goes along with that email address such as:

- Full name

- Business name (if you are a B2B business)

- Age/Birth date

- Date they first purchased from you

- Historical purchasing data (amounts, products, etc)

- Services they've used

- Mailing address

- Parental status

- Marital status

- Gender

The more data you have about the individuals in your email list, the higher quality it becomes because you are able to segment the list based on that data. Consider the value of segmenting your email list in the following scenario:

You have an upcoming store-wide sale coming up. You want to highlight some great deals on a few of the more notable products. You will have have one of these options:

- If you do not have enough data to segment your list, you will have to pick the products you think will appeal to the most people on your list and send the same email to everyone. Some will be more likely to appreciate the email, while others might see the sale as irrelevant and begin to think that your store is not for them as much as they thought. You might try to combine both categories of products into one email, but then run the risk of not appealing to either crowd as much as possible.

- If you do have data and can segment your email list based on age for instance, then you can send the younger crowd products that are geared to them and likewise with the older crowd. This will increase the effectiveness of your email campaign as well as help your customers see your store as their store.

Data helps you personalize your marketing efforts and make them more effective, but you have to do the homework up front. Implement processes and systems to help collect that data. If you are relying on sales reps or technicians to collect the data, make sure they are well trained and have the tools they need. There are several options for software and hardware that can help you collect this data.

Email Content:

If you have a great email list with a lot of data, then you are in a good position to really have a profitable email marketing campaign. The only thing that's missing is great content! You don't get too many chances to prove to your email list that you're worth paying attention to. If they get the hint that you're being super salesy or annoying there is a good chance they will hit that unsubscribe button or filter you out of their inbox for good.

That's why you want to make sure the content in the emails you send are worth reading. However, before you can get them to read what's on the inside of your email, you have to grab their attention with a good subject. Keep in mind that a conversion is the culmination of several 'small sales'.

Every time you influence the decision of a customer, it's a small sale. Your goal is to influence them all the way to the cash register. Having a great brand is a small sale that helps them trust you. Having a great subject line is a small sale that gets them to open it. Think through the types of things that will grab your customers' attention. Be true to your brand, your customer, and the content inside the email. It only takes one "You've won a free gift card" bait and switch email campaign to lose a customer forever. The subject line should accurately reflect the personality of your business, be creative enough to catch their attention, and (if the content in the email is compelling) staying true to that content will be easy. Consider the pairs of subject lines below. One clearly states what the email might be about, the other makes it more likely that the recipient will actually open it:

- Local Fitness Gym

    - Boring: "Membership Updates"
    - Interesting: "Unlock Your Potential: Learn about the new features available in your membership plan"

- CPA (Certified Public Accountant)

    - Boring: "Quarterly Tax Newsletter"
    - Interesting: "Navigate Tax Season Like a Pro: Insider Tips!"

- Pediatrician

    - Boring: "Health Clinic Information"

- o Interesting: "Little Heroes Newsletter: Your Guide to Keeping Kids Healthy!"
- HVAC Company

  - o Boring: "Annual HVAC Services Reminder"
  - o Interesting: "Beat the Heat/Cold! Don't Forget to Schedule Your Maintenance"

In Holistic Email Marketing, Kath Pay argues that emails can be reused just by changing the subject line. We have found this to be an effective strategy to get more opens on an email campaign. Most email platforms will allow you to resend an email campaign to people on your list who didn't open the email the first time it was sent. Changing the subject and making note of which users open which subjects can help you determine how to grab their attention better in the future. Consider using words that cater to different emotions in your subjects, curiosity, fascination, excitement, exclusivity, and encouragement are some places to start.

"If people simply look at the subject line and delete the email, a subject line written for the long-term gain will leave a little bit of branding and value behind - the nudge effect in action." - Kath Pay, *Holistic Email Marketing*

If you can make the initial small sale and get them to open your email, the body of the email should be another small sale. Think through the action you want your customers to take. Have a goal for your email campaigns. The goals should directly inform the calls to action (CTA) in your email. Some CTAs are:

- Clicking a link/button to go to a specific page on your site where they fill out an inquiry form or purchase a product.

- Calling to use a discount code to place a reservation before a certain day

- Reminding them of an upcoming deadline (tax filing, subscription ending, or a scheduled service) and prompting them to take an appropriate action.

Some emails can simply be informative or entertaining and you should have at least a few of these in your email campaigns every year. These can be something as simple as a "Happy Holidays" message with a picture of your staff, to announcing a new team member, to letting people know of an update within the business (that new branding or website perhaps?). Before you send any email campaign, put yourself in the shoes of your customers and ask yourself, "would I want to read this email if I were them?" If the answer is yes, hit send. If it's not, then revise it.

Email Technology

There are hundreds of email marketing platforms available to small businesses today. Mailchimp, Constant Contact, Emily, the list goes on and on. And the quality and prices are wide ranging, and in this particular case, low-cost doesn't necessarily mean low-quality. Look for a software that:

1. Has a user-friendly email editor that will allow you to easily create and edit high-quality email campaigns. This is typically a WYSIWYG editor (What You See Is What You Get) that will allow you to add images, text blocks, and other modules via drag and drop. Different platforms

offer different bells and whistles for their editors, but most offer similar functionality.

2. Track the open and click rates of the recipients. This is one way you can tell whether or not your email campaigns are working. Make sure your email marketing software has a reporting dashboard where you can see how many recipients open your emails or click on various links with the email. This is important data that can inform future email campaigns and your marketing in general by letting you know what people are most interested in and what sort of things close those small sales.

3. Integrates with other elements in your martech stack. Your martech stack is simply the set of technological tools that you use to assist you with marketing. Your email marketing can play an important role in your marketing automation. Being able to trigger emails that are sent a day, week, or month after a purchase can be a valuable instrument in your marketing tool belt.

4. Allows your list to be segmented. To take advantage of the data you are collecting, you will need to be able to segment your list and only send certain campaigns to particular customers in that list. Some platforms call this segmenting, some call it tagging.

5. Allows you to export your contact list. If you aren't using any other sort of database to store your client contact information, then this is especially important. If you ever decide to not use your email platform any longer, then you will essentially lose your hard-earned email list if exporting is not allowed.

For more info on email marketing technology scan the QR or visit theclimb.guide/email

Pitfall Warning:

Marketing technology is constantly changing and there will always be a new shiny object that martech companies will try to dangle in front of your face. However, stick to your strategy, no matter how shiny the object is. Pursuing the latest and greatest in technology often results in several hours and sometimes several hundred dollars or more lost in setting up the new thing only to find that it really didn't move the needle for you.

However you implement your email marketing, keep these words from Kath Pay in mind:

"Before you select a single image, write a line of copy , or think about subject line, you must know what you want your email message to achieve. Then every element of your email message must support this objective."

After Eva and her dad had a big piece of her 3rd month anniversary cake, the reality of what she was up against was starting to become clear. The shop had barely broken even over the last few months. She was really beginning to doubt whether the money she had invested in her advertising was worth it, now she had a looming deadline to make the Aurora Nightshade launch a hit, and she didn't know where to start. She tried not to show the panic she was feeling inside.

As a way to channel her anxiety, she started digging through boxes and office supplies in the back room in search of the business cards from the chamber ribbon cutting. She knew they were back there somewhere. She had every intention of setting up an email database in that first month, but as things go with small business ownership, there were bigger fires to tend to. But now, this was a fire. She needed to get the news out about the new product release and sending all those contacts an email would help it get in front of the connectors in the community just in time for the holiday shopping season. "None of them are probably Shadow Stalker enthusiasts," she thought to herself, "but they might know someone who is. It's not a lot, but it's worth a shot."

"Aha!" she exclaimed as she pulled a stack of business cards bound in a rubber band out of a drawer. If anyone had been watching her closely, they would have noticed a profound exhale, as if she was releasing the weight of her worries in that moment. She clutched the cards to her chest for a moment and with some forced determination, jumped back into action. By this time, Chris had shown up for his afternoon shift. She came from the back office and set the stack of cards in front of him as he put a bite of cake into his mouth.

"Don't hate me," she said ominously. "I need you to enter all these into our customer database." His mouth full of cake made it hard to object, but he managed to make a puzzled expression. Before he could ask, she added, "Oh, and we need a database."

Chris swallowed his cake as quickly as he could to say, "About that... I was able to get into the old website. Evidently there was a newsletter signup form on there at one point and there were about 500 emails collected there. I downloaded them as a CSV file," he said as he pulled a thumb drive out of his pocket and placed it on the counter between them. "They might not all be valid anymore. They could have been sitting there for 10 years or more. I.."

Eva interrupted him, grabbing his shoulders with a look of glee on her face. "Chris! You're a genius! Thank you!" She said, grabbing the thumb drive and nearly skipping to the computer. She plugged it in the usb port and waited for it to show up in the Finder window.

"I saved it as 'emails.csv'", Chris said as he shoved another bite of cake in his mouth.

She opened the file and saw a spreadsheet appear with names and email addresses. She scanned down the list and saw several AOL and Earthlink email addresses. It was old, but it was worth a shot. Between this list and the chamber business cards they would have about 600 email addresses. "Not a bad start" she thought to herself.

CHAPTER 14: THE FINAL ASCENT

That night she sat in bed and poured over notes that had been collecting on her desk at the shop and spreadsheets detailing as much of a sales history as she could pull together from the last few years. She compared how different product categories had ebbed and flowed, how many Shadow Stalker products they had sold and when. The document that gave her the most anxiety was her P&L statement for the year to date. With the holiday season approaching, the toy vendors had required prepayment on the inventory that should be coming in the next month which she had to put on credit. They were also going to have to pay for the inventory of all the new Shadow Stalker figures, but at the pace they were going, they might not make it up before the end of the year.

Trying to keep a business in the black was a new sort of anxiety that she did not anticipate last year. Back then she was having fun planning fall weekend getaways and planning upcoming holiday get-togethers. Now, she was up, trudging through the minutia of running a small business.

She remembered the goals she had set out 6 months ago to conquer wrote them in large bold letters with a Sharpie:

- *15% increase in Shadow Stalker sales from last year.*
- *Increase daily in-store visitors by 20%*
- *See at least 10% of monthly sales from repeat customers by year's end.*

Taking the time to reflect on her goals and where she was at with them, made her realize how little she had done since she had started this journey. As she looked them over again with all the sales history in front of her, she began to get a better grasp on where she was at with her goals. She began to think through what had worked, what might be working, and what were some opportunities to capitalize on.

Year to date, Shadow Stalker sales were down about 10% compared to the same period last year. Even so, they were still the top seller of any single product series. So far this year, they had brought in a little over $6,000 or about $750 per month. Last year, total, they sold around $13,000 with a major portion coming through the holidays. To meet her goal this year (of $14,950), she would need to more than double her sales over the next 4 months, plus meet the goal of selling 200 Shadow Stalkers. Even with the holiday surge and the new product launch, this was no small feat.

Over the last two months she had implemented a system to track foot traffic. She and Chris would both tally the number of adults and children coming through the door on a notepad throughout the day and then enter the numbers in a spreadsheet as part of their closing routine. She was encouraged to see that the foot traffic was on an upward trend from the beginning of July until then. She was also excited to see some patterns of what days had heavier traffic than others. However, she still hadn't figured out a good way to calculate repeat customers. She had considered coupons or a rewards system, but she really needed to implement a better POS that would do some of that automatically for her.

Amongst all her documents and spreadsheets were random notes, to-dos that never got to-done, and questions that sprung up throughout the day that she didn't have the time to answer at that moment. As she looked over those notes, these are some of the questions and insights that stood out:

- Why are people looking at their phones so much during their time in the shop?

- Average sale amount has decreased over the last few years. How can we increase it?

- On the weekends, there is a steady amount of foot traffic downtown, but there are too many families with young children passing by. How do we get them to stop in?

- Are my brand awareness ads working?

- What do my customers think?

It was getting late and Eva's brain was fried. Mentally, she was exhausted and knew that a good night's rest would allow her to refocus in the morning. She knew they had to act quickly to get Marley's on a path to success. She also knew that she needed input from her whole team if they had any chance of pulling this off.

She typed out a text message to Chris, "Sorry for the late text! Can you come in an hour early tomorrow? We need to brainstorm! I'll bring donuts".

She knew her dad would be in early because old habits are hard to break. She packed up her notes and papers and set her alarm an hour early to give her time to prep the back room at the shop for their brainstorming session.

Before turning off the lights, she got a ding on her phone. It was Chris. "You bet! See you then. Can you get one with sprinkles?!"

The next morning Eugene, Eva, and Chris gathered around the old wooden table in the back of Marley's. The air was thick with anticipation and a hint of anxiety. Sprinkles fell into Chris's hand as he took advantage of Eva's donut bribery. Eva began, her voice steady yet imbued with a sense of urgency, "First, let me say that we aren't in a bad place, but we aren't in the place I want us to be."

Seeing everyone's faces turn from anxious to serious goaded her on to get to the point. "Before I decided to take over Marley's, I set out some goals." She flipped over the first sheet on the big sticky note board she had picked up that morning, to reveal the three goals. She gave them a moment to read them over before jumping back in. "We also need to add a new goal to this list that helps us get to goal #1: sell 200 Aurora Nightshade toys. By my estimation, this means that we need 300 Shadow Stalker sales in all between now and the end of the year to meet goal #1."

Chris, rubbing the back of his neck, winced a little at the lofty goal, not wanting to verbalize his concern. Eugene, always the optimist, chimed in, "That's more Shadow Stalking than I've ever done in a holiday season, but we've faced bigger mountains before. This is just another adventure for us!"

A look of calculation had come over Chris's face as he jotted something on a notepad. Eugene and Eva watched as his face contorted into a few different expressions before saying, "If I am reading your numbers right, then we have been averaging 22 Shadow Stalker sales per month. To get 300 Shadow Stalker sales by the end of the year, that means we will need about 75 per month, or 2.5 per day."

With eyes widened, Eugene let out a low, impressed whistle acknowledging the task's magnitude.

"We can do it," Chris continued, "but we need a plan. A damn good one."

Mustering as much leadership as she was able, Eva jumped in with a smirk and an air of determination, "And that's why I've called you here today."

"I have made a list of some questions and notes I've taken while working in the shop. I think it might be a good starting point to help us develop a plan. Feel free to add your own too." Eva ripped off the large sheet that listed their goals and pressed it against the wall so that it was displayed for the whole team. Underneath that sheet was another that had these things listed:

- Are people using the shop to 'showroom' our toys?

- How can we increase the average sale?

- How do we get people off the sidewalk and into the store?

- Is the advertising working?

- What do my customers think?

She went ahead and ripped that sheet off the pad too before sticking it to the wall. The crew took a minute to process the notes.

Respectfully, Eugene raised his hand as if he were in class. "Yes Dad?" Eva said, slightly rolling her eyes at his formality.

"What do you mean by 'showroom'?"

Chris jumped in with his hand raised, "Oh! I know this one, can I answer it?"

Eva jokingly scolded him for raising his hand, "You guys, I am not a teacher. Stop raising your hands. There are just three of us, let's just have a good solid discussion, a debate if we have to. I want us to get the best plan possible and I need you both to be as creative and honest as you can be for the next hour or so." Her passion for the shop and her trust in her team were equally on display.

Chris jumped in. "Showrooming is when someone goes into a store like ours and checks out the product before ordering it online. They use us as the showroom for the online store. And yes, I think they are," he said as one bringing the news of an approaching army to a general. He explained further, "I have seen them looking at products online while they're in the store, but in their defense, they might also be looking at reviews of the products."

Eva raised her eyebrow and nodded. She hadn't considered that as a possibility before.

Eugene chimed in, "What if we preempted them?"

Eva and Chris both gave him a quizzical look. He explained, "You know, what if we cut off their need to get on their phones? We could give them the ratings and reviews on display with the product." Chris and Eva looked at each other, with an expression of surprise and respect for such a simple yet innovative idea from Eugene.

"Don't act too surprised," Eugene said defensively. "This old gray head has a few tricks left up his sleeve."

Chris added, "You know, we were actually talking about this in my behavioral economics course the other day. It's called the social proof heuristic. It's like a mental shortcut people use to make complex decisions. Instead of trying to figure out if their kid will like a toy, they just look and see that 1000 other people's kids love the toy and so it makes the decision easier for them."

"This is great you guys!" Eva said. "I am going to add it to our idea list," she said as she jotted "display reviews and ratings on products" on a blank post-it note. "What about our average sale, how can we increase it?"

"That's easy, we could just raise our prices a little, right?" Chris asked.

"I wish!" Eugene responded. "Our prices are already scraping the ceiling. If we raise them anymore we are going to drive people away!"

Chris was able to recover from the mild embarrassment of his ignorance of the pricing situation and followed up with, "Well, is there a way to just get them to buy more things?"

"I used to have candy near the checkout," Eugene reminisced. "Talk about increasing a sale! That used to work like a charm, but

I eventually pulled it because evidently giving kids a lot of sugar is frowned upon these days," he concluded with a solemn look on his face.

"Well, sugar might be bad, but I am sure there are some other small things we can generate some impulse buys with. Chris, can you research some small products that we could sell for $5 or less in the checkout area?"

"Sure thing!" Chris responded enthusiastically.

They sat in the back room, silent and deep in thought, each of them looking from one post it note to the next and rolling ideas around in their heads. Eva knew that she had to respect this time and not rush it, so she willed herself to not interrupt the moment.

Chris broke the silence, "What about bundling products? If we could get someone to buy 2 or 3 things when they would normally just buy one, then that would increase the average sale."

"Fantastic idea, Chris!" Eva said as she wrote "product bundles" on the note pad. She was encouraged to see the energy and progress of this process so far and nudged them along, "What else?"

Eugene had been ruminating on why less people were coming into the store when they were already downtown. He couldn't help but think that kids being hyper focused on their devices and less curious about the world around them was part of it. They weren't pulling on their parents' sleeves to come into the shop anymore and some parents were fine with that.

He spoke up and focused everyone's attention on #3. "We need to grab their attention somehow. All these kids do is keep their noses stuck in a phone these days. We have to figure out a way to make them look up and see the world and see how magical it can be!" Eva and Chris could sense the emotion behind Eugene's plea. The world used to be much simpler. At one time, children were able to find joy in creative toys and books much easier than they do today.

"Eugene, something you said gave me an idea," Chris continued, "If we want to get their attention and show them how magical the world can be, why don't we bring in a magician!?" Chris's face was now beaming at the thought of a master of illusion dressed in a tailored coat with long tails and a top hat catching passersby as they walked through downtown, wowing them with their sleight of hand, and ushering them in the store, and pointing them to the magic trick section.

This time, Eva and her dad exchanged glances of approval. Eugene jokingly said, "Not bad, young man." Eva, performing some quick calculations in head, said "If we could hire a magician for $100 every Saturday at the busiest 4 hours, and they were able to bring in 4 new customers, then I think this idea could work. Chris, do you think you can find a good magician for $100?"

"It's worth a shot!" Chris replied.

"All right, I am adding another task to your to-dos, Chris," Eva said as she added "Magician" to the post-it note of ideas.

Eva looked at the clock, it was almost 10, time for the shop to open. She didn't want to end their brainstorming session without attempting to answer #4 on their list. "OK, before we have to wrap this up... the million dollar question: Are our ads working?" she asked them, hoping for some profound insight that could guide her next steps.

Eva's father chimed in and reassured her, "Eva, this place has seen more people coming through that door since you've been steering this ship than we've seen in years." He continued, "I don't know if it's the ads or just the fact that people are happy to not have to deal with this grumpy old man anymore, but something is working." She appreciated her dad's encouragement, but she was also frustrated that he didn't see that even though they were getting more customers, they were also paying more staff and spending money on advertising, something they hadn't done significantly in the past. Right now they were nearing the end of her dad's initial loan to get things off the ground. If they were going to stay on track, they were going to have to figure out a way to keep new customers coming in and old customers coming back. Understanding whether her marketing was working or not was critical in this process.

"Thank you Dad, but this question is really important to me. Right now we don't have money to waste on advertising if it's not working. And I don't know how to tell if it is or not."

Meanwhile, Chris had been working intently on something on his laptop. He turned his screen around and said "See if this helps!" Eugene and Eva both examined the screen closely. It didn't take long before a similar confused expression appeared on their faces.

"What exactly are we looking at?" Eva asked him.

"Glad you asked!" Chris said proudly, "This is your Google Analytics account."

"Oh! I've heard of this!" Eva exclaimed. "Web Monkeys told me about this. So... what exactly are we looking at?"

"Great question. You are looking at your Search Console Report in Analytics. I have it filtered to show the number of searches that have the word 'Marley' in the search phrase," he explained.

Eva and Eugene had huddled more intensely around the screen this time, looking at a line graph that had a steady angle from the bottom left to the upper right indicating an upward trend in the results.

"What you are looking at is a graph of those searches. You can see the number of 'Marley' searches on the Y axis and the daily date on the X axis."

Eva and her dad's eyes started to glaze. "English, Chris." Eva said, pulling him back into the world of the nontechnical.

"Oh, sorry," Chris said, shifting gears. "What this means is that more people are searching for Marley's by name."

"So, what you are saying is that our the influencer marketing and social ads are starting to work?" Eva asked.

"Exactly!" Chris continued, "This shows us that more people are interested in what Marley's is, where we are, when we're open, or what we offer."

Eva examined the angled line with a number in the corner signifying the increase since the last month, "+33%", and felt a sense of pride and possibility.

Eva looked around the table at her father and Chris. There was a tangible sense of optimism between them all. "Good job team," she said, proudly. "It's almost time to open up shop. Let's start working on these things as we can and plan to have a full game plan by the end of the week. Also," she continued, "we have one more big hurdle to jump before we can breathe easily: The Aurora Nightshade launch. This is our chance to put Marley's on the map in the greater Burlington area. We've got to knock it out of the park. Can you both do another early morning tomorrow?"

Chris grimaced, "I have 2 midterms this week, and this is really my only free day."

The Shadow Stalker launch was going to be here before they knew it and Eva knew every second counted to make this a successful launch. "Well, this is important. We will just have to close early this evening so we can knock this out."

About that time, the color started to fade from Eugene's face and he grabbed the edge of the table. "Mr Marley, you don't look great," Chris said.

"I just need to sit down."

Eugene grabbed the chair near the work table and pulled it over to sit down. "Dad, are you ok? What's going on?" Eva asked with a sense of urgency.

"I just need to catch my breath. I'll be ok," he said.

"Chris, will you manage the shop until I get back? I am going to take dad to the doctor." Her concern grew when her dad didn't argue with her. "Of course," Chris said solemnly. She grabbed her coat and purse, helped her dad up, and walked with him out the back door where her car was parked.

After Eva ended the call with the doctor's office, letting them know they were on their way, Eugene said, "Well kid, you're doing something right. There's lots of excitement at Marley's these days.

More excitement than this old man can handle evidently." He reached over and squeezed her hand. The fear and anxiety over her father's health mixed with the stress of the shop, which in turn added a layer of guilt for worrying about business when her father's health was at risk. All she could do was return his gesture and hold his hand firmly.

Eugene sat in the sterile doctor's office under the harsh white lights, Eva by his side. The room, with its clinical ambiance, seemed to amplify the gravity of the doctor's words. "You must understand, Eugene, your health requires serious attention. It's crucial to minimize stress and manage your workload more effectively," the doctor urged, her tone both compassionate and firm. Dr Garza was small in stature, but she had learned early on to speak with authority and to detect the slightest hint of dismissiveness in a patient's response to her, which would be met with a swift realignment of perspective if needed. She had probed Eugene about his work habits over the last six months, learning that he had not taken it as easy as he had been prescribed initially. She checked off some boxes on the paper on his clipboard and scribbled a prescription on the small pad he pulled from his pocket.

"Mr. Marley, if you want to be around to see your daughter make an empire out of the toy shop, then you need to do what I am telling you." Her face was firm and unyielding. Eva looked at her dad and saw the rare vision of submission and humility that mortality thrusts upon a person. "Go home, rest and don't report for duty at the shop until you come back here in a month and I give you the clear."

"Yes, Doc," Eugene says respectfully as she handed him the prescription and instructs him to take the medicine twice a day.

"And I will see you in about a month too," she said to Eva. "My grandson loves Shadow Walkers and he heard that Marley's was going to be the only place carrying that new one."

Despite the weight of the current circumstances, it brought some hope to Eva to hear that word was getting out about the launch, even without them trying. She forgave Dr. Garza's fumble on the name, and told her she couldn't wait to meet him.

The drive back home was reflective and subdued. Eugene stared out the window wrestling with his desire to be in the thick of what was happening at the shop, but also realizing he needed to trust Eva with it. The minimal conversation meandered from business to family, from past struggles to future aspirations.

Eva helped get her father get settled at his house before leaving to return to the store. "Call me if you need anything at all, OK? Nothing is too small," she told him, concerned and feeling guilty for leaving.

He gripped her hand. "Evangeline, promise me you'll keep Marley's thriving, no matter what."

Her response was immediate and unwavering, "I promise, Dad. You've built something incredible, and I'll do everything to keep it growing."

Eva sat in her car for a moment to collect herself. She knew there wasn't anything she could do for her dad at the moment, but it didn't make the thought of leaving him any easier. She promised him that she would keep Marley's thriving, so she wiped her eyes and put the car in drive with a new determination.

When she got back to the shop, she found the door locked and the sign on the door that said "Be Right Back!" She gave

Chris the benefit of the doubt. By that time it was a little after 2. "Perhaps he's grabbing a late lunch," she thought. She unlocked the door and took the sign down, before texting Chris, "I'm back.".

She received a quick reply, "How's Eugene?? I'm almost back. I have an idea! Don't mind the mess in the back. I'll explain."

She went to the back room to hang up her coat and saw paper and trimmings on the table that they had planned around earlier. There were several rectangles of various sizes with quotes printed on them. On the rectangles there read things like, "The story was full of twists and turns, heartbreak and romance. I won't spoil anything, I cried at the end." and "My two toddlers can't stop playing with them!"

About that time, Chris came through the back door with his hands full. "Hey!" he said, cheerfully. "I assume your dad is ok, since you're back here?"

"Yes," she said as she watched him heave two bags of frames and other supplies onto the table. "He's just suffering the consequences of being a stubborn old man. The doctor told him to stay out of the shop for a while. Too much activity and stress until his heart heals more."

Chris looked a little sad and empathetic. He enjoyed Eugene's company and knew his health was a heavy weight on Eva as well. "We're a man down and a big challenge is in front of us," Eva said, trying to change the subject.

"What do you have going on here?" she asked.

Chris's expression turned quickly to excitement as he explained, "You know that idea we were talking about with having the reviews and ratings next to the products? These," he said, gesturing to the stack of uncut paper and the little rectangles, "are all the reviews! And here," he said lifting up his bags, "are the frames!"

Eva admired Chris's initiative. She was also glad she had hired someone with good taste as she looked in the bag to see frames that would look great on the shelves. "Great job Chris!" She said with a genuine look of gratitude. "Let's see what they look like on the shelves!"

They spent a few minutes cutting and placing the quotes in the frames before hauling a handful out to place them on the shelf. The notes, printed in a handwritten font, and tucked amongst the array of books and merchandise, served as tangible connections to the thoughts and feelings of fellow readers. This ingenious approach seamlessly bridged the digital divide, creating a more authentic and grounded shopping experience that Eva was certain would resonate with customers.

By that point, the sun was starting its descent and it was golden hour in downtown Burlington. Eva heated up some coffee in the microwave in the back, before sitting down at the table ready to plan the big event. The store was quiet, a stark contrast to the whirlwind of ideas about to unfold. They were alone, save for the silent company of books lining the shelves, witnesses to the birth of a new chapter in Marley's story.

Eva, with her eyes reflecting a mix of determination and creativity, looked at Chris. "This event isn't just a launch; it's our statement to the world," she began, her voice steady and inspiring. Chris nodded, his expression serious yet sparked with excitement. He knew the stakes were high, but the potential was even higher.

They started with the guest experience. "Let's transform Marley's into an immersive world," Eva suggested, her hands gesturing vividly. The idea was to create an environment that would transport visitors straight into the heart of the Shadow Stalker series.

Chris, ever the practical thinker, chimed in, "We'll need mood lighting, themed decorations, maybe even a soundtrack that resonates with the series' ambiance."

Eva's eyes lit up at the suggestion. "And what about a photo booth or a backdrop for pictures? Guests could take pictures with props from the series." The idea was brilliant, a perfect blend of fun and engagement.

"Let's do it," Chris agreed, his mind already racing through the logistics.

The conversation shifted to marketing. "We should leverage social media heavily," Chris proposed, tapping a pencil against his notepad. "Teasers, countdowns, maybe even a contest leading up to the event."

Eva loved the idea, knowing the power of anticipation. "A contest could create buzz," she said, thinking aloud. "Maybe a chance to win an exclusive Shadow Stalker merchandise bundle?"

As they delved deeper into the plan, the room became a crucible of creativity. Eva mentioned interactive elements. "Let's have a scavenger hunt during the event, clues hidden in book passages," she proposed, her voice tinged with excitement.

Chris agreed, adding, "It'll engage the guests and make them explore the store more."

The discussion about merchandise was next. "We should have exclusive items available only during the event," Chris suggested, his mind keen on exclusivity driving sales.

"Limited edition copies, special artwork, things like that." Eva nodded, already visualizing the display. "And let's not forget bundles," she added. "Book and merchandise combos at a special price for the event."

A few hours had ticked by, the store bathed in the soft glow of evening, their plan began to take a concrete shape. Eva paused, looking around the store, her mind envisioning the event. "This is going to be more than just a launch party," she said, her voice a blend of pride and anticipation. "It's a celebration of what Marley's stands for – a love for stories and community."

As the planning session drew to a close, the store was silent once more, save for the soft rustling of papers as they tidied up. They had laid the groundwork for an event that promised to be a milestone for Marley's, a testament to their hard work, creativity, and dedication to bringing stories to life. With a final look around the store, Eva and Chris stepped out into the night, their minds filled with visions of the event to come, a night where the magic of Marley's would shine brighter than ever.

As the crisp air of autumn danced through the streets, a palpable energy began to emanate from Marley's over the coming weeks. A vibrant transformation was underway. The store, under Eva's guidance, was evolving into more than just a retail space; it was becoming the beating heart of the community, a magical nexus where tales spun from the pages of books intertwined gracefully with the reality of everyday life.

After his midterms, Chris reengineered the checkout area so that there was a small aisle designed with a captivating display of carefully chosen items awaiting their customers before they made their purchases. These were not just ordinary products; they were thoughtfully selected keepsakes, each a gateway to the fantastical realms and adventures nestled within the store's books. Elegant bookmarks, whimsical key chains, and a myriad of other small yet enchanting treasures along with collectible cards and small pocket-size toys lay within easy reach, inviting customers to make spontaneous purchases as they waited at the checkout counter.

Amidst this bustling scene of change, a new figure had emerged, becoming an integral part of Marley's charm and allure. Kyle, an enigmatic character with a flair for the theatrical, was a man of average height but with a presence that filled the room. Clad in a coat of the deepest blue that rippled and shimmered like a twilight sky, he captivated onlookers with his bright, mischievous eyes that seemed to hold secrets from other worlds.

His performances were a masterful blend of classic sleight of hand and clever, engaging banter. Coins would mysteriously appear from behind children's ears, only to vanish and reemerge in the most unexpected of places – hidden within the creases of a book nearby, or playfully perched on the shoulder of an amused customer, much to the delight of the watching crowd.

One interaction, in particular, stood out as a testament to the magician's skill at creating moments of wonder. A young boy, barely eight years old, stood transfixed by the magician's antics. Noticing the boy's awe-struck gaze, the magician invited him closer with a warm, inviting smile. "Would you like to witness something truly remarkable?" he asked in a voice that was both intriguing and gentle.

The boy, his face a canvas of excitement and curiosity, nodded eagerly. The magician, with a dramatic flourish that seemed to make the air around him shimmer, produced a deck of vibrantly colored cards. "Pick a card, any card," he urged, his voice imbued with an element of mysterious fun. The boy's small, excited fingers selected a card, his anticipation palpable.

As the boy clutched the card, the magician embarked on a series of elaborate, mesmerizing gestures, his hands moving with a grace and fluidity that suggested they were weaving spells rather than performing tricks. With a final, grandiose wave, he asked the boy to reveal the card. It was an unassuming number card, but the magic lay in the detail – the number perfectly matched the boy's age. A collective gasp of delight rose from the assembled onlookers, followed by a round of heartfelt applause. The magician, with a knowing wink, remarked, "Magic is not just in the grand gestures; it's in the little coincidences, the numbers, the stories we cherish and share."

Parents, witnessing this enchanting exchange, were more inclined to stay, to explore the wonders of Marley's, leading to more browsing, more conversations, and, inevitably, more purchases.

From her vantage point, Eva watched these magical interactions unfold, her lips curled in a contented smile. The magician, with his enthralling performances, had not only drawn people into the store but had also infused Marley's with an atmosphere brimming with joy, laughter, and a sense of endless possibility. It was precisely the kind of magic Marley's needed – a sprinkling of wonder in the mundane, transforming everyday shopping into an extraordinary experience. And it only took a few weekends of Kyle capturing people on the street and directing them inside for Eva to realize that they needed to get a larger inventory of magic tricks. The few kits and small tricks that they had were selling faster than they could keep them stocked. With the holidays coming up, she decided to double her usual inventory and added a few new tricks on top of that.

In addition to these enchanting performances, Eva had masterminded another hit – the introduction of bundled products. These weren't mere combinations of items; they were thoughtfully assembled collections that offered customers not just value but an immersive journey into their favorite stories. Each bundle was a celebration of the narratives they sold, a way to foster a deeper sense of connection and belonging among their clientele. Fans of the Shadow Stalker series and other popular titles found in these bundles a tangible piece of their beloved fictional worlds, making them irresistible.

Throughout this flurry of activity and innovation leading up to the Aurora Nightshade launch, Chris stood as a beacon of resourcefulness and unwavering commitment. Balancing his demanding academic schedule with the rigorous needs of the store, he was a constant presence, often staying well into the night. His dedication to Marley's was evident in every carefully crafted plan, every strategy meticulously laid out. His tireless efforts ensured that every aspect of the store's transformation and the upcoming event was executed flawlessly.

Eva, ever observant of the efforts of her team, especially recognized the monumental workload Chris was shouldering. Chris was the backbone of their guerrilla marketing as well. He was always looking for good photo ops of people to use for social media, had built a decent following on TikTok primarily from trends he would recreate with the action figures in the store, and was diligent about collecting email addresses, cell numbers, and reviews from customers. Their Google Business Profile now had 57 five star reviews and was consequently showing up higher and higher in organic searches. Wanting to acknowledge his extraordinary efforts, she planned a small but meaningful gesture of appreciation. One evening, as the day's work was winding down and the store bathed in the soft glow of twilight, she approached Chris, a small package in hand.

"This is for you, Chris," she said, her voice imbued with sincere gratitude. "Your dedication hasn't just been noticed; it's been the backbone of all we've achieved these past weeks." Handing him the package, she watched as he unwrapped it to reveal a limited edition collectible Raven Blackwood from the Shadow Stalker series – a rare and coveted item.

Chris, usually a paragon of composure and focus, was visibly touched. A look of genuine surprise and gratitude illuminated his face, a rare moment of vulnerability that spoke volumes of the depth of his commitment to Marley's. "Thank you, Eva. This means more than you can imagine!"

In the weeks leading up to the eagerly anticipated Halloween event, it became clear that Marley's had undergone a remarkable transformation. The store had blossomed into a hub of creativity and connection, a place where the joy of discovery and the thrill of imagination were celebrated daily. It was no longer just a bookstore; it was a vibrant community space, a haven for those who sought not just to buy books but to experience the magic woven within their pages, to connect with others who shared their love of stories, and to be part of a narrative that extended far beyond the confines of its walls. Marley's had become a destination.

As the week leading to the Shadow Stalkers event progressed, Eva juggled her excitement and the flurry of preparations. Earlier in the week, a heartening update had come from Dr. Garza. Eugene, adhering to the doctor's advice and showing improvement in his health, had been cleared to attend the event. It was a reward for his 'good behavior,' a term Dr. Garza playfully used to commend his adherence to her guidance. This news had brought a spark of joy to Eva's heart.

The day of the event arrived with a promise of magic and celebration. Eugene, fully embracing the spirit of the occasion, decided to surprise everyone, especially Eva. He had chosen to dress up as the enigmatic magician from the Shadow Stalkers series, a character he found particularly intriguing. His costume was elaborate, complete with a deep blue cloak that shimmered in the light and a mock wand that he wielded with a mischievous glint in his eye.

When Eva arrived to pick him up, she was greeted with a sight that brought laughter and delight. "Dad, you look incredible!" she exclaimed, her eyes shining with amusement and affection.

Eugene, in his magician attire, twirled around, enjoying the moment. "Thought I'd get into character," he said with a chuckle. "I figured it's not every day you get to be a part of something as special as this."

Together, they set off for Marley's, Eugene's spirits lifted and Eva's heart warmed by her father's enthusiasm. The night ahead promised to be unforgettable

As evening fell, Marley's transformed into a realm straight out of the Shadow Stalkers series. The store was alive with people dressed as their favorite characters, the air buzzing with excited chatter and laughter. The dimmed lights and thematic decorations created an otherworldly ambiance, perfect for the launch.

Staci, who had helped create the new Marley's brand, arrived in a stunning costume, her presence turning heads. She found Eva amidst the crowd. "Eva, this is incredible! You've outdone yourself," she exclaimed, her eyes wide with amazement.

"Thanks, Staci. It's a team effort," Eva responded, her pride in Marley's evident.

Ethan, another familiar face, made his way through the crowd, his costume impressively detailed. He approached Eva with a wide grin. "Never thought I'd see Marley's like this. You've really pulled off something special," he said, shaking his head in wonder. Eva smiled, grateful for the support.

The highlight of the evening was the arrival of Dr. Garza with her young grandson, both in costume. The boy's eyes sparkled with excitement, taking in the magical world around him. Dr. Garza approached Eva. "Thank you for inviting us, Eva. It's a night he'll always remember."

Eva beamed, "I'm just glad you both could make it."

As the night progressed, the costume contest took center stage. Participants strutted on an improvised runway, their outfits a testament to their love for the Shadow Stalkers series.

The creativity and effort put into each costume were met with cheers and applause from the audience. Eva, serving as one of the judges, felt a sense of community and belonging that went beyond just selling books.

The event reached its peak when the limited Aurora Nightshade figures, a centerpiece of the launch, sold out. The demand was overwhelming, and the excitement palpable. Customers proudly held their purchases, their faces glowing with satisfaction. "We did it, Chris," Eva whispered, watching the scene unfold.

"We really did it," Chris replied, his voice filled with a mix of relief and triumph.

As the event drew to a close, Marley's was a beautiful mess. Streamers lay strewn across the floor, empty snack plates dotted the tables, and the once neatly arranged shelves were in disarray. But the chaos was a small price to pay for the success of the night. The team, though exhausted, shared a sense of accomplishment. They had turned Marley's into the talk of the town, a place where stories came to life.

Eugene, who had watched the event unfold with a mix of awe and pride, turned to Eva. "You've made something truly special here, Eva. I couldn't be prouder," he said, his voice thick with emotion. Eva hugged him, her heart full. "It's all thanks to you, Dad. You started this story, and we're just continuing it," she replied.

The night was more than just a launch event; it was a celebration of passion, creativity, and community. It was a night where the magic of storytelling brought people together, creating memories that would linger long after the last guest had left.

Marley's, under Eva's leadership, had become a beacon for those who cherished stories and the worlds they opened up.

As the last guests departed and the team began the cleanup, there was a sense of contented fatigue. The laughter and chatter of the night echoed in the now-quiet store. Marley's, with its doors closed and lights dimmed, stood as a testament to what could be achieved with a vision, hard work, and a love for stories.

The Shadow Stalkers event was more than a success; it was a milestone. It was proof that even in a world increasingly driven by digital experiences, the charm and allure of a physical space filled with stories and dreams could still draw people in. For Eva, Chris, and the rest of the team, it was just the beginning. There were more stories to tell, more events to host, and more dreams to weave into the fabric of Marley's.

As they locked the doors, leaving the mess for tomorrow, they stepped out into the cool night air, their hearts full. The night had been a whirlwind, a beautiful, chaotic dance of light, color, and emotion. And it was worth every moment.

CHAPTER 14: THE FINAL ASCENT

CHAPTER 15: THE SUMMIT

Eva woke up to the sounds of kids playing in her neighborhood. For a moment, she panicked, thinking she had overslept on a Saturday. She blindly felt for her phone on her nightstand and brought it close to her face to read the screen without her contacts in. 9:05, January 5 - Monday. She heard the distinct sound of plastic scraping against ice and realized that the atypical Georgia blizzard had hit and the kids were enjoying their extra day off for the holidays.

She was also glad that she wouldn't have to worry about too many parents trying to return unused sleds they had bought the week before in preparation for the winter storm. Stocking up on the sleds was Chris's idea, even though her father had warned that he had done that before in the past and it took 4 winters to sell all the sleds he bought when the forecasted 8-10 inches and 30 degrees turned into rain and mid-40's. After a successful holiday season, they were all feeling a little optimistic though.

Eva decided to close the store that day due to weather and focus on running the numbers for the 4th quarter. She made a full pot of coffee, because she knew she would be spending the day well into the afternoon in front of her computer. She had tried to keep up with whether they were meeting their goals through the fall, but the holiday season hit full force and while she knew they were making a profit, she hadn't had a chance to sit down and figure out exactly where it all came from and where it could be improved for next year. The bank account was definitely fatter than it had been when she started, but she also had a stack of unpaid bills to sort through. She sat down and logged into the various websites that housed all the vitals of the business: accounting, inventory, analytics, social media, email marketing, and every other system that had any numbers to look at. She started with the things she could figure out easily... number of sales, average purchase amount, best-selling products, worst-selling products, what months and weeks had higher than average sales, etc.

Next to her computer she had a piece of paper with folds, grease marks, and coffee cup stains competing for real estate with the words written in bold permanent ink:

- *15% increase in Shadow Stalker sales from last year.*
- *Increase daily in-store visitors by 20%*
- *See at least 10% of monthly sales from repeat customers by year's end.*

She knew that the first goal had been met. After the launch party and the Black Friday and holiday push they made that featured Aurora Nightshade, they had sold out of the Shadow Stalkers inventory repeatedly. However, that victory still felt fresh to her and the dopamine rush from looking at those numbers hadn't faded yet. So, she filtered her sales by the category labeled 'Shadow Stalkers' and saw the final result for the last year: $17,596.43, over $3,000 beyond her goal. She basked in the glow of at least one victory for a moment, reflecting on all the memories over the last six months.

The second and third goals were a little harder to determine since she had really only been tracking those numbers for a few months. She pulled up the spreadsheet that they had been using to track in-store visits. There were obvious ebbs and flows around the launch party and the holidays. To get a more realistic assessment of their progress, Eva filtered out the outliers (Halloween, Black Friday, and Christmas Eve) and saw that the upward trend they had started from July to October had continued through the end of the year. The month to month increase in foot traffic of July compared to December was an increase of 22%! This was great news and it was definitely reflected in the total sales, but Eva wasn't sure how much they could expect to keep seeing an increase like that. She jotted "how much more daily foot traffic can we expect?" on a new notepad.

The third goal had frustrated her over the last few months. They had attempted to track repeat customers by sending out an email with a coupon, but they still only had a limited number of email addresses. She had her email system pulled up and saw that they had sent out an average of 300 coupon codes a month since October. She then pulled up her book keeping software and filtered by discounts. They only had 30 redemptions total, an average of 3% return. She wondered if the coupon wasn't a good enough incentive, but also worried about discounting too much.

With the rush of the holidays, they didn't have the chance to replace their POS with a better system. She knew that if they could easily capture email addresses and phone numbers, it would boost their email marketing. She added "Replace POS" to her list and underlined it three times. She looked at her email and coupon redemption numbers again, wondering if she was missing something. She finally resigned to the fact that goal #3 didn't get met. "Well, two out of three ain't bad," she said to herself.

She looked through all her other numbers to make sure things were on track before getting up to refill her coffee. As she was pouring another cup, her mind wondered to the future. What would this year look like, what sort of goals should she set, what new adventures would Marley's Home for Wayward Books and Gifted Toys encounter?

She felt her phone buzz. When she checked the screen for a notification, she saw it was an email from Bill at Shadow Stalkers. The subject read "FWD: The End of an Era." Curious, she clicked the notification and it opened up the full email:

Hey Eva,

Happy New Year! Congratulations again on an amazing rookie year at the shop. I hate to be the bearer of bad news, but Shadow Stalkers got bought out by OmniComics at the end of the year and just announced that they are shutting down the toy division. I am forwarding the email from the corporate offices. I'll still be around for a bit, but I am also looking for some new opportunities. Let's keep in touch!

Eva looked up from her phone and stared blankly out her kitchen window. Shadow Stalkers was a huge part of their revenue this last year. "This changes everything," she thought to herself. This was a big blow, especially since they were expecting to see some big gains off the notoriety in the Shadow Stalker community that the launch party had garnered them. She felt the momentum they had worked so hard over the last few months grinding to a halt.

Perhaps it was the spirit of the new year or maybe it was the joyful sounds of the kids playing outside. Either way, the optimism of her dad kicked in and she could hear him saying, "We've faced bigger mountains before. This is just another adventure for us!"

With that mindset and a little more caffeine, her entrepreneurial spirit kicked in and she began to dream of what the future holds for the Marley's team.

EPILOGUE

The next year had many ups and downs for Marley's, not the least of which was the discontinuation of Shadow Stalkers.

Luckily, Eva was able to ride the wave of the product sunset, holding some of her inventory back in order to get a premium for them once they became more valuable as discontinued collectibles. She also spent that January determining which direction Marley's would go without their flagship toy product. If she had learned anything over the last several months, it was that nothing is guaranteed and that you have to be ready to roll with the punches of operating a business. Nothing is guaranteed. It was with that spirit that she brainstormed several possibilities for the next phase of Marley's. She finally landed on the idea of creating a party and class room in the heretofore unused back room in Marley's. It was overcrowded with random things that had collected there over the years and needed a good cleaning, but it was an untapped asset for the business.

With the success over the last year on the books, Eva was able to secure a loan from a local bank to help renovate the space and create an area that parents and kids alike loved for themed birthday parties. Part of her plan was to partner with her new magician friend and a local artist to offer magic and art classes in the space.

She catalogued the space's transformation over social media and used her growing email list to help launch the new space. It didn't take long for reservation inquiries to start rolling in. She worked with Web Monkeys to implement an ecommerce system for parents to sign their kids up for classes. The first magic workshop sold out within a few days.

While parties and classes helped increase the bottom line and broaden her services, the absence of Shadow Stalkers was still a threat and there weren't many products that rivaled the popularity of Shadow Stalkers. So, she leaned more heavily into their wide array of unique toys and thoughtful book collection. Shadow Stalkers helped get her conquer the mountain of relaunching the business, but she realized that she didn't need it to help her conquer the new mountains ahead.

"I have found that crafting a personality around your brand that people can relate to has been key for Marley's," Eva told a friend who was thinking about starting her own business. "Having that strong brand gives me lines that I can stay in between and it takes the uncertainty out of a lot of my decision making. It helps me stay focused on long term vision of what I want Marley's to be."

Over the next year, Marley's had to deal with the occasional business struggle, like figuring out a new point of sale system and making sure their bookkeeping was accurate, but over all, the new year was a steady success.

Early in the following year however, Eugene's health took a turn for the worst, which prompted some changes for Eva's family. Her brother, Michael, and his wife decided to move closer to Burlington to help care for their aging father. Christina, Michael's wife was able to find a job in nearby Atlanta quickly and so Michael chose to take some time off from his IT career to help get the kids settled into their new life and be spend some time with Eugene. One day, while the Eva, Eugene, and Michael were having dinner, Eugene goaded Michael about his work and encouraged him to help Eva out at the store - "like old times" he said.

The three of them were enjoying a slice of pie and coffee to round off the evening.

"You know..." said Eva, pausing with a look on her face that betrayed the wild idea that was about to follow. "Marley's is in a great position to open another location." Both Michael and Eugene's eyes widened. "And Atlanta would be the perfect spot for a hip and quirky book and toy store brand." Eugene looked at Michael like Eva had just lobbed a hot potato to him and was waiting for him to send it back.

Michael chuckled a little to try to shrug off his sister's idea, but it had hit him in a way that he couldn't have expected. He paused, looking down at his coffee. Eva felt like she was in one of those high stakes interviews that you see in the movies where she just slid over a piece of paper with a number on it and was waiting for her brother's reaction. However, if it were a piece of paper it would surely have less zeros than the ones in the movies. His face scrunched a little. Both Eugene and Eva were on the edge of their seats. They couldn't tell if it was good or a bad scrunch. He opened his mouth only to close it again a few times, only adding to the anxiety of the moment. Finally, he said simply,

"It's not the craziest idea you've ever had, Eva," looking over at her with a grin and eyes that said "what are you getting me into?"

She punched him playfully in the arm for pushing her buttons the way only a brother could, and let them all break the anxiousness of the moment with laughter. Eugene looked at them with eyes glowing and said to himself, "Another adventure for us Marley's."

Over the next few weeks, Eva and Michael began mapping out the details with meticulous care to make sure one or both of them could be with Eugene as much as possible for doctors visits and other needs. Chris had taken on more responsibility at the shop, which allowed Eva to be away more so she could also help with some of the technical details of opening up the new location.

The next six months were a blur. They were able to find a space for lease in an older part of downtown Atlanta that fit the personality and brand of Marley's to a T. Between Michael and Eva, they were able to take out a loan to renovate it and make it exactly what they needed, complete with wood-trimmed windows and doors and wooden book shelves with a library ladder that gave it a nostalgic and timeless air. She had learned so much from relaunching Marley's that a lot of opening a new location gave like second nature. She made connections with the Atlanta chamber and some of the local civics groups and began reaching out to the city schools to see how they could collaborate with teachers. When the day finally came to open Marley's Home for Gifted Books and Wayward Toys in downtown Atlanta, Eva, Eugene, Michael, and his whole family gathered with in front of a red ribbon. Eva handed over the over-sized scissors to Eugene, who, with tears in his eyes, cut the ribbon to the applause of all around.

Eva had already conquered many mountains. But now Marley's was a multi-location retail store, and she knew this would be the tallest mountain yet.

ABOUT THE AUTHOR

Jeremy LaDuke started Epic Nine Marketing Outfitters in 2013 and has helped hundreds of businesses from local startups to national CPG brands find the right route and the best tools to get them to the top of their marketing mountains. He has helped start multiple nonprofit organizations in Blount County Tennessee, including the Sky City Entrepreneur Center, the mission of which is to help local business starters thrive.

Almost everyone who has read Climb before this publication has asked if they will get to learn about the future of Eva and Marley's in a sequel. If you want to join those inquiring minds, scan the QR code below to sign up for updates on future publications, find links to Epic Nine, and receive regular marketing updates.

The Marketing Trailblazers Podcast:
Fireside Chats with Mountain Conquering CMOs.

Whether you're sipping your morning coffee, commuting to work, or winding down after a long day, let the Marketing Trailblazers podcast be your guide and companion in your marketing journey. Dive into a world of captivating conversations, enlightening lessons, and the inspiring tales of mountain conquering CMOs. Together, let's blaze new trails in the world of marketing! Scan the QR code below to find links to the podcast on your favorite podcast app.

marketingtrailblazers.com

www.ingramcontent.com/pod-product-compliance
Lightning Source LLC
Chambersburg PA
CBHW030500210326
41597CB00013B/742